Living Beyond Rainbows

David Marty

iUniverse, Inc.
Bloomington

iUniverse books may be ordered through booksellers or by contacting:

iUniverse
1663 Liberty Drive
Bloomington, IN 47403
www.iuniverse.com
1-800-Authors (1-800-288-4677)

ISBN: 978-1-4502-8227-7 (sc)
ISBN: 978-1-4502-8228-4 (hc)
ISBN: 978-1-4502-8229-1 (ebook)

Printed in the United States of America

Library of Congress Control Number: 2010918876

iUniverse rev. date: 12/22/2010

Contents

Dedication

This book is dedicated to my dear friend Esther, who helped me navigate through midlife and infected me with her self-esteem. I also dedicate the book to Art, my partner, who put up with me through all of my challenges. Finally, I want to dedicate this book to all the people who've had to deal with the HIV virus and who've added to the sea of humanity with their common knowledge of how to live and survive and coexist with HIV.

Foreword

AIDS has been on the radar since the 1980s. It spread far and wide throughout the world because in the beginning, its full impact on human health wasn't fully understood. Early on, there was fear, apprehension, and misinformation surrounding AIDS. There were many on the religious right who tried to demonize HIV. Some of that still exists today.

As time went on, AIDS brought a profound depression to a once thriving and vibrant gay culture. My best friends and acquaintances alike had their lives shortened, and a lot of the gay contribution to the social fabric of life became muted. Advances have been made, but so far, the cure has proved elusive.

As a volunteer from the beginning, I had a unique position of observation to watch improvements in life expectancy and quality. I learned the hard lesson that it sometimes takes only one thoughtless exposure to HIV under perfect conditions to make a permanent change in a life. I discovered that I was positive in 2006. While I knew a lot about AIDS before my diagnosis, I am now keenly aware of transmission modes and the attributes of HIV. I'm also more aware of the stigma that surrounds HIV. Now, as I near sixty years old, I finally realize that life is a gift. No one gets off the planet alive. We're all mortal humans. So we must make the most of each and every living day that we have.

HIV is a virus. Fortunately, it's not highly contagious. One can't get AIDS from shaking hands, kissing, or hugging. But there's still a lot of fear and apprehension out there when certain people encounter someone who's known to be HIV positive. There are growing numbers of people who're alive and struggling with their health because of HIV. If you don't want to get AIDS, all you have to do is insist on protection while having sex or when handling body fluids (e.g., blood, vaginal or seminal fluids) of strangers. Of course, abstinence is always protective. A strong sense of self-worth and self-esteem may ultimately be the very best protection against HIV.

I've found that the harshness of my current medications isn't helping me to reach my goal of healthy longevity. I've opted for a different protocol, which seems to work for me. I don't endorse this for everyone. It seems to work well for me to be medicated one month and not the next. Perhaps it's my destiny to find a way to successfully thrive even while HIV is cohabiting my body. Others are also trying to do the same thing. Maybe a better way to think of the AIDS virus is as the parasite that it is, which we must learn to coexist with. Someday, perhaps a cure will be discovered. I hope so.

In the meantime, we HIV-positive people need hope and compassion rather than judgment and scorn. Ignorance and insecurity only seems to breed more fear and isolation. Open up the blinders and get educated. Realize that we're all in this sea of humanity and that we all benefit when we learn to love and respect each other. That begins when we learn to love and respect ourselves.

Life is a gift. Go beyond fear and explore your world while you're still able.

Forgive yourself and learn to love yourself so that you're able to love others. The world is big, but when you learn to love and respect one another, it can become a more manageable place.

Acknowledgments

I need to thank so many people in my life who've helped me and encouraged me to continue writing this book. Jean and Louise eagerly helped me to make the book more readable. Thank you to my many patients, who inspired me to keep writing. My thanks and gratitude to my "benefactors," who helped me financially when I was in such need and who introduced me to Master Lin. And I add a special thank-you to all my friends and the members of Aliveness Project, who've help me by example.

Introduction

My name is David. I'm an adventurer. I have a young restless spirit. I've never liked the constraints of having limits arbitrarily imposed on me. My many childhood heroes include Davey Crockett, Lewis and Clark, Superman, and Dorothy of Kansas. One goal in my journey through life is to maintain my youth. I'm a gay man and a chiropractor, and I'm trained in natural healing.

My father was a chiropractor as well, and I was brought up outside of the mainstream medical establishment. Even before I knew that I was gay, I was made aware that I wasn't quite good enough. My parents, who probably also struggled with low self-esteem, reinforced my academic achievements and provided wholesome nutrition for my body but failed to nurture my self-respect. When I discovered I was gay, I felt alone. Without positive role models and with mostly scorn from the "straight" world, I was faced with charting my own course.

Another goal of mine used to be to live a healthy life all the way to 120 years old. Now a goal of healthy longevity seems less limiting. Being gay creates some added dilemmas regarding aging. Some milestones along the road are missing. Marriage and children are often missing, and social recognition is usually conditional. There are only a few older role models. Because of AIDS, many of my contemporaries are gone. Perhaps most importantly, self-esteem may be frail, which makes growing up gay a struggle. Gay culture has long considered youth and virility a big part of its foundation. As one ages, peer support seems to wane. Amid this backdrop, midlife can be a real challenge.

I first found myself in gay culture when I was nineteen years old. At that time, I looked at thirty-year-olds as old. It's funny how things change along the way. For me, the road through midlife seems to be the bumpiest. One is forced to confront the realities of life's journey and to accept and assess progress or the lack of it. I'm intelligent, brave, adventurous, and sometimes I can come off as self-assured. However, my family, religion, and cultural nurturing all failed to instill a strong sense of self. Low self-esteem left me vulnerable to self-destruction. I believe that sometimes I chose to hide my lack of self-respect by overachieving and taking daring risks in order to try to earn respect. On my journey, I've used my magical thinking, determination, and perseverance to boldly forge ahead, often ignoring or diving through the usual barriers.

We're sometimes fortunate enough to rub elbows with someone who's already blazed the trail. It's comforting to know that even though it may sometimes feel lonesome, we're not alone.

I prefer to live beyond the usual limits. One of my guides for my journey is a woman named Esther. She's an older person with generous limits and a youthful spirit.

Esther seems to inoculate me with her own self-esteem. Sometimes she reminds me of the Wizard of Oz.

Chapter One

The Rainbows

I don't know about you, but sometimes life comes at me so fast that all I have time to do is to react by reflex. After years of feeling as though I'm always swimming against the current, I feel an ominous quiet as I pause to rest my weary body. Suddenly I become aware that I'm being sucked into an eddy, which is pulling me ever closer to the headwaters of a giant waterfall. I know that I'll soon be going over Niagara Falls without so much as a barrel to protect me.

Without any knowledge of how much power the falls holds and how far the drop will be nor what to expect at the bottom, I ready myself to take the plunge by tucking my head and pointing my toes. Just as I've approached most challenges in my life, at a certain moment, I dive head first over the edge of the falls, into the thunderous water. During my descent, I experience an overwhelming feeling of being powerless. I've no idea what to expect when I reach the bottom. I've made the leap; now I try to relax, just speeding headlong down into the abyss.

I reach the bottom sooner than I expect. Alternately I hold my breath and then gasp for air. My lungs feel like they're going to explode. I land in a deep pool of cool, clear water. As I swim to the calmer reaches of that pool, I realize that I've joined legions of other people in the giant sea of humanity. I stare at all the others, and I blush because they're all naked. Then Esther Williams swims up to me and invites me to join everyone in a massive display of a synchronized water ballet. I look over to where the water crashes on the rocks, and I see that the bright light is being fractionated into beautiful rainbows by the misty water droplets formed from the pounding water.

I assess my body for the effects of my unscripted plunge and note that for all the rage of the waterfall, I'm relatively unscathed. I've only a few minor bruises and cuts, from which I know I can easily heal. It's now time to coexist with the rest of humanity. I join the rest of humanity in a ballet of naked synchronized swimming.

That's how I'd summarize my life using my magical thinking.

Chapter Two

Esther

I woke up to start a new day. All of the turmoil of 2006 was finally winding down. I was feeling like I was finally a part of humanity again. I wasn't just alive, but I was starting to grow strong after nearly dying in intensive care. My first priority was to reestablish some of my obligations, especially those that I had to Esther. She and I visited regularly for years, and then I abruptly stopped seeing her in the nursing home when my energy gave out.

Now again, I am visiting Esther, who is the oldest patient in my practice. I have known her for several years and have watched her on her final road toward eternity. Esther is ninety-five now, and for the last three and a half years, she has lived in a nursing home. She is still alert and friendly, especially with me. Esther has outlived her money. She's in the best home that the state of Minnesota can pay for.

I usually visit Esther almost every week. After years as my patient, we are also good friends. I am one of only a few people who come to visit her. She is mostly bedridden now. She has a devoted son, Charles, who also visits nearly every day. When he is unable to visit, he calls his mother on the phone, sometimes more than once a day. Esther is a little hard of hearing, and I have to speak loudly to her. I'm usually quite soft-spoken, so it was an effort for me at first. But Esther's worth it.

I've been told many times that as a doctor of chiropractic I shouldn't even accept cookies as a gift from patients. I think the rules are way too limiting and overly strict, and I like to work and live outside the box. When Charles first called me to ask if I would see his mother professionally in the nursing home, I gladly accepted and mentioned that my fee would have to be forty dollars. I agreed to visit and give Esther a one-hour massage while I hooked her up to a portable Alpha-Stim machine. It was about all I could do for Esther these days. She was getting even frailer each time that I visited her. The Alpha-Stim was supposed to help synchronize her brain waves and reduce stress and anxiety and help with pain management.

Not too long ago, Esther was moved into a different room. Her former room came with roommates, but she kept outliving them. She often knew that they would not last very long when she first met them. Esther seemed to always be in touch with her surroundings. She was polite and regularly complimented her caregivers by name, even those who recently came from Africa. Of course she had a few people on her list that she didn't like. She never hesitated to tell me about their bad manners.

Together, we decided Tuesdays just after lunch would be a good time for my visits. It was usually pretty slow for me that day, and I could make it to and from the nursing home without much traffic. The fall of 2006 was a sort of rebirth for me. That was the year that I nearly died. I felt eager to climb the steps and enter the door from the stairwell, which had an alarm on it. I had learned long ago how to disarm the door, and I walked past the staff desk. Usually no one was on duty. When there was someone, they were already familiar with my comings and goings.

This time, I had to ask at the nursing station, "Where is Esther now?"

I got to the new room at the end of the long hall. It was a corner room. I noticed that there was one empty bed and another one with an old woman lying in it. At the far end of the room was Esther's bed. I was excited to see her because she always knew how to convey to me how valuable my visits were for her. The other woman was only about ten feet away, and she appeared to be in a deep sleep or a coma. I closed the cloth curtain between the roommate and Esther. I went to Esther's bed and gently touched her arm. She smiled and opened her eyes at the same time.

As usual, she said, "It's good to see you again." The next sentence was, "What's new in your life?" and then, "How is Teddy? and "How is Harold (Art)?" After so many visits, Esther had a lot of her conversation memorized.

This time I had something I was anxious to tell Esther.

I answered, "Everyone is fine, thank you. What's new is that I've decided to write a book." I waited to see her reaction.

Her eyes brightened and she asked me in a tone that was matter-of-fact, "What's your book going to be about?"

I loudly blurted out, "I'm going to write a book about my life, my life story."

As Esther thought about it a little bit, a voice from the comatose woman rang out. She said very authoritatively, "Who cares?" The voice continued, "It's not worth writing. Nobody will care to read it."

I was stunned. I thought, *What a mean old lady!* I wanted to pull open the curtain and yell, "You won't be around to read it anyway!" I hoped that Esther hadn't heard her, and I wondered if it was maybe my own subconscious feelings of inability that had created the vocalization.

I don't think Esther heard the other woman because she soon responded.

She said, "I think a book is a good idea." Then she added, "Your book is bound to be very interesting."

I was relieved. I've always considered myself more of an artist with many talents, and I was easily intimidated by harsh criticism. Esther was the first person to whom I divulged my ambition of writing. Her approval was more important to me than the opinion of an old woman who would not be alive to read the book anyway. It was my conversations with Esther that led me to feel that we all have books within us and how important it is to sit down and actually write things down.

* * *

Backgrounds

Chapter Three

Preliminaries

The first time Esther came to see me was in the fall of 1993. She called me and walked over to my office, which was four blocks away. She was a matronly Norwegian woman, who was slightly plump but fairly agile for her eighty-two years. Another older woman in her building referred her to me. Esther lived at Tree Tops, a senior building that was part of Walker Senior Care. Esther had lived in the neighborhood many years. She was familiar with and unafraid to explore all the amenities. She wore a cheap brown wig, and the first few times at my office, she was reluctant to take it off.

* * *

Nineteen ninety-three was a pivotal year for me. I was only forty-two, but I felt as though I was having an early midlife crisis. Shortly after the New Year, I learned that my mother had breast cancer. My father was a chiropractor of the old school. He honestly believed that chiropractic and his own skills, with the help of God, could overcome all of life's illnesses. My mother was devoted to him and was very subservient to him, especially when health issues were involved. Dad waited until the tumors in Mom had invaded her abdomen and choked her internally, shutting off her esophagus and preventing food and water from getting into her stomach. At that point, he became so alarmed that he drove her to the Mayo Clinic in hopes of a miracle.

The miracle was never going to happen. All of us children knew that something was wrong at Thanksgiving. There are six of us—three boys, three girls. I am the fourth child and middle boy. We four who lived closest to Mom and Dad sat down that day to discuss our concerns. None of us thought cancer back then. We thought that maybe Mom's diabetes was to blame for her failing health. If Dad knew anything, and I am sure he knew more than any of us, he wasn't offering us any answers. We quizzed Mom about her blood sugar levels and her medications, and everything seemed to be in order. We put aside our immediate concerns.

Chapter Four

Summer in Europe

After a few early visits to my office, I asked Esther, "Have you traveled very much in your life?"

She beamed when she said to me, "Well, I'm planning to visit my brother Calvin in Seattle soon."

Years before with her first husband, she moved to California for a short time. She hated it. Her husband didn't work very much and drank a lot. Esther finally told him that she was moving back to Minnesota, and he could come with her or stay; it didn't matter for her. He moved back with her, but a few years later, he died of heart problems. With her second husband, she traveled once to Norway and Denmark. Every time she mentioned that trip, she dwelled on the wonderful cheeses and pastries that she sampled there.

She got excited when she spoke and said to me more than once, "The cheeses in Denmark are delicious. I bought some cheese and fruit and a big loaf of bread, and Harold and I went to the park and had a real picnic."

* * *

I told Esther about my trip to Europe over the course of several appointments. My trip was in 1970 and lasted all summer—four months. I started in London and hitchhiked my way to Wales and Scotland before crossing the channel and touring continental Europe. I spoke French. I had three years of high school and one year of university French under my belt. I went from Northern France

11

to Belgium, Holland, Germany, Denmark, Austria, Italy, and even Yugoslavia. I took a train from Rome all the way to Auch, France, near Toulouse. From there, I walked to Lavardens and started a four-week archeology dig. I signed up for this work back in Minnesota as a work-study program.

Walking the dirt road, I rounded a bend and saw Lavardens in the distance. The castle was prominent on the horizon, surrounded by fields of sunflowers in bloom, all with their heads pointing to the sun. It was magical. I worked with a lot of French high school and older kids and with a few English and Italians. We worked two weeks at a seventeenth-century castle. A Belgian couple recently purchased it. They wanted it restored enough to have light and sound shows there. The other two weeks were spent at an eleventh-century abbey in the town of Moirax. We were moved from the castle because there were vicious sand fleas in the lower part of the castle, where we slept. We woke up with welts on our bodies from their bites.

Moirax wasn't much better when it came to pestilence. It was a small town of about sixty inhabitants. We took over the town hall. After the first night, the girls of our group opted to sleep outside in the stable with the boys because they could hear rats gnawing in the floors and walls of the town hall, where they were trying to sleep. We put cantaloupes on the windowsills overnight to ripen, and they would be gnarled garbage by morning after the rats got to them.

I had fun in both of these tiny villages. I was able to speak French fluently, and the people of both villages told me I was the first American they'd seen since World War II. Once, when it was my turn to be on cook duty, I saw all the cornfields surrounding Moirax. I inquired at the grocery store if it was possible to get a few ears of corn. For me, it was August and time to eat sweet corn.

I spoke French to the owner of the store. I said, "Bonjour, madame. It will soon be my turn to cook for our group. I was wondering if you could get some corn for me to cook the way I am familiar with in the United States."

The woman owner seemed confused and asked, "What kind of corn do you want?" She laughed and then continued, "The corn grown here is for the pigs and geese, not for people."

I said, "I really want some corn to cook for our group."

Then she asked, "Do you want mature corn?"

Unfamiliar with the different corn stages in French, I answered, "Yes."

The next day, I went again to see what she was able to come up with. She assembled twenty ears of last year's corn, totally dried up and ready for the geese.

I said, "No, the kernels should be soft and mushy."

She told me, "I cannot get corn like that."

Next, I went directly to the farmer. He was so handsome I almost became tongue-tied. He was blond and blue eyed and extremely virile looking and about thirty years old. I had a few people from our group with me.

I asked, "Would it be possible for us to pick about fifteen to twenty ears of corn right from your field?"

He repeated, "I grow my corn for the pigs and geese."

I told him, "Yes, I know."

He agreed to let us into his field and said, "You may pick some corn as long as you don't destroy the field while doing so."

So my Midwest boyhood favorite, corn on the cob in August, was finally going to happen. I cooked the corn in a huge pot of boiling water. Because it was field corn, I added both salt and sugar to the water and boiled it longer than usual. Some of the group really liked it, some thought it was tough and difficult to digest, and a few were neutral. My surprise came the next morning as I was pushing the little local kids in the wheelbarrow; several of the women of the town approached me one by one and asked me for the recipe for the corn. Everyone had heard about it, and they were all anxious to try it. I wonder if they still eat it today, forty years later.

After working in France, I hitchhiked to Spain and Portugal before returning to Paris. From there, I flew back to Minnesota. In Europe, I had my very first encounters with homosexual men.

My European travels opened up my life. I had traveled several different cultures and countries. Often alone, I frequently camped near main roads, and at the end of each ride, I would just lay my sleeping bag down in a field and sleep soundly until dawn. I was a fearless teenager and lived on sardines, cheese, bread, and yogurt. Every new ride was a different experience. Before I reached home again in Minneapolis, I realized that, of course, I was gay.

Chapter Five

Boston Memories, Chiropractic College

One thing Esther and I never talked about was my volunteer work with people who had contracted the AIDS virus. Even when I was going through chiropractic college, I had an uncomfortable feeling that the euphoria of coming out along with the dazzling disco was all going to crash. Before chiropractic college, I spent '74 and '75 living in Boston. I moved there after graduating from the University of Minnesota with a degree in International Relations. For several years, I rebelled against the family preoccupation with chiropractic. My father, two uncles, and my brother had all gone into the field. After my return from Europe, I wasn't sure that a gay chiropractor would even be accepted into the profession.

Two years in Boston allowed me to have space to sow my wild oats and to contemplate my career future. I sowed enough oats to form a new subsidiary to Quaker. Once, in the free VD clinic in Boston, I was given a questionnaire to fill out. I needed to answer it before they would give me a shot of penicillin for gonorrhea. I stumbled over the question of "How many different sexual partners have you had in the last year?"

I was amazed that anyone kept track of such things and why it was any of their concern. I had to do some fast calculations. There are 365 days in a year. Half the time, I didn't want to have sex for a variety of reasons. Other times, however, I sometimes had anonymous sex with three, four, five, or six people in one evening.

Before AIDS, we didn't consider protection. The worst thing to happen would be getting VD, which I got twice in Boston. I was a virile twenty-three-year-old. I put down 190 sexual contacts in the past year to try to be conservative. Fortunately I was given the shot in my buttocks and that was that.

I moved to Boston in the fall of '73 so that I could be there when my infatuation at that time, Kevin, moved there. We met in Minneapolis, but he said he wanted to live in Boston. He wanted to attend Boston University to study architecture. I moved out there with my two friends, Michael and Glenn. We got an apartment and started mixing into life as Bostonians. About six months later, Kevin flew from Minnesota to join me. He and I moved to a different apartment, which we shared with Alan and Dana. Alan was about as flamboyant as a gay man could be. Dana was a nerdy paralegal. They were a couple because Alan needed financial support, and Dana enjoyed the flattery that Alan gave him.

When Kevin and I finally moved to our own apartment, it was to 82 Commonwealth Avenue. We had a penthouse apartment. There were basically two large rooms with a kitchen, a bathroom, and an entry hall. We barely had furniture except for my king-sized waterbed that was unheated. We sometimes laid naked on the rooftop of the adjoining building, which was one floor lower than our apartment, so we could tan. It was a six-floor walk-up, and we learned fast not to leave without every essential thing. It took a lot of effort to have to go back for anything. It was also infested with cockroaches. They sometimes crawled over our faces at night. That took some getting used to for us. Neither of us had ever seen them before.

There was also a problem with heat in the winter. The Lebanese landlord had the heat on some sort of timer, and the heat went off at midnight and on again at six in the morning. The waterbed got really cold, and the two women living next door to us showed us frozen glasses of water next to their bed. Finally, just a couple of months before I moved back to Minneapolis to go to chiropractic college, the plaster fell off of a large part of the living room ceiling.

My infatuation with Kevin came to an abrupt end when I discovered during a physical argument that he actually got sexually aroused when he was spanked and beaten. It was a sexual turn-on for him and a major turnoff for me. We started going our separate ways after our first year together in Boston. Before that time, we shared many great times. We would pal around a lot, but we had different work schedules and different fantasies. We went to Provincetown in the summers. We also played around sexually with other gay singles and couples. We loved to dress up in our bellbottom pants and platform shoes and go out to dance the night away at The Metro near Fenway Stadium. Our favorite song was "Don't Rock the Boat." Every time it was played, we looked for each other so we could dance together.

I left Boston to go to chiropractic college. My parents drove from Minneapolis with a trailer to pick me up and take me home. It was in the days of deprogramming, and my parents tried their version of that. I think they influenced the minister to give a sermon on the prodigal son the Sunday that we returned from Boston. My mother discovered marijuana in my pant pocket when she was doing the laundry after that trip. Now I was a proven criminal. They banished me to their lake home and told me to contemplate my life. Before long, I found an apartment and a car and my old job and soon started another four years of college.

Chapter Six

Chiropractic as My Vocation

Esther was always so cheerful. It wasn't contrived but truly genuine. She talked to me about how she met a man in her building and how they became good friends. Esther never mentioned it, but I immediately suspected that her male friend was gay. He worked at the old Schlamps and sold furs. Then he retired and moved to Esther's building. Those two became pals and did many social things together. Around 1990, he died and was buried in Lakewood Cemetery. Esther talked about it because my house was just across the street from where he was buried. She sometimes went to visit her friend, who was now in the grave.

Esther didn't care about the sexual inclinations of people. She looked through them and found the kernel of humanity, which constituted good or evil. She didn't like self-centered, egotistical, selfish people. Even at her age, she was an adventurer, and she was very comfortable having good experiences with well-meaning friends. Esther hated gossip and complained to me that so many of the old ladies in her building spent their days in idle chatter and hearsay. She sometimes joked with them and told them she was visiting her boyfriend when she was really coming to my office. I liked to encourage her with that fantasy.

In many ways, we had something stronger than just a doctor-patient relationship. At first it was sharing close information with each other. Esther was always interested in life. Money wasn't her priority, and it wasn't mine either. My joy was in making people feel better. I went to work every day with my mantra, which I repeated to myself almost daily—"To be the best healer that I could possibly be and to pay attention to details no matter how small so that I could help with the problems my patients came in with."

* * *

I tried to work in corporate America and realized it wasn't for me. It was in Boston that I discovered that the family trait of healing existed in me. As friends came over to visit, they would sometimes complain of headaches or discomfort and asked for an aspirin. Growing up, I never had aspirin, and even now, I have never bought aspirin or Tylenol or any OTC painkillers. So I would tell them to lie down on the carpet. I gave them an adjustment like my father used to give me. Almost always, it was effective. After thinking about it more and more, I decided that this could be the passion that could rescue me from New England Bell, my best job in Boston. I had rebelled long enough, and I decided to succumb to the family destiny and become a chiropractor.

It wasn't just the idea of healing others. I was curious to know as much as I could about my own body. I also looked at my father and his colleagues and noticed that most of them were fairly healthy into old age. I thought of being a dentist but gave the idea up after thinking about what it would be like to stare into open mouths all day and breathe in bad breath. I also searched and discovered that dentists have the shortest life spans of all the healing professions. I thought that being a chiropractor would also help gain some approval from my family. On that last point, I was wrong.

Even after I was finally in practice, my brother Dan said to me one day, "You will never be successful because God doesn't reward a homosexual lifestyle."

Apparently God does reward those who go to church regularly, even if it is mostly to promote themselves or to reward those doctors who make patients come back often, until the insurance runs out.

During my studies at chiropractic college, I was forced back into the closet when another guy who I thought would be a friend told me he wasn't going to hang out with a queer. I went through four years of college unable to talk about my private life to anyone except my closest personal friends. I lived in an apartment with Michael, the friend with whom I previously moved to Boston, and Ruth. Ruth was pregnant at the time, and I think my parents were hoping that the baby was mine too, but it wasn't. Ruth eventually became a sister-in-law to Michael. My worried parents sent a minister to the apartment to check on me. Ruth was about seven months pregnant and showing it. When the minister arrived, I had just taken a few hits of marijuana. I was so surprised to see this man. He didn't sit down but stood in the long hallway and questioned me about my faith and lack of church attendance.

He said, "Your parents are concerned because you don't go to church anymore. They think you are ignoring your upbringing."

I said to him, "I work all day Saturday and Sunday to pay for my schooling and apartment, and I don't have time for church." Then I added, "I still remember my catechism and prayers."

* * *

While in school, I studied hard but always with the intent of being an artist. Chiropractic was magical for me. I really believed that the laying on of the hands was a powerful healing force. I'd lived my whole life with the benefits of good chiropractic care. I wanted to know as much as I could about my own body and how I could help others. I paid my own way through school just as I had at the university. I worked thirty or more hours a week while going to school full time. I had little time for a social life or television.

I went to work at the same produce company, which I left when I moved to Boston. It was hard physical labor with long hours especially on the weekends. There were rats, bats, cold temperatures, and hot temperatures. It was a huge old warehouse with fluorescent lights dangling from twenty-foot chains, which hung down from the ceilings. I finally ended up quitting after the boss refused to give me a raise. Next, I had a temporary night job putting together plastic housings for a popular Christmas toy. That lasted two weeks. I lived for a month on soybeans, and I fixed them every way that I could think of. Now I hate soybeans. Finally I got a job as a waiter, and when I was fired from that restaurant for no fault of my own, a much better restaurant hired me. I stayed there until I graduated. As a waiter, I always had money in my pockets, but I got bored when the job became too predictable. I didn't like serving unhealthy food to unhealthy people.

Many of my fellow students assumed that chiropractic was genetically instilled in me and that I didn't have to study. On the contrary, I was somewhat dyslexic, and I had a terrible time getting through the thick medical textbooks. I reverted back to the days when I was a teenager and read most of the classics. I had to actually live in the books to understand them. This wasn't too hard when reading *Tom Jones, A Tale of Two Cities, An American Tragedy, The Brothers Karamazov,* and *Don Quixote*. It was a lot harder when reading books about gynecology, neurology, cardiology, etc.

I had a disagreement with my microbiology teacher. She had been a Catholic nun. I was unfamiliar with the viciousness some of them possessed. She outlined the course from the beginning and assigned certain pages to read from the huge textbook. Almost weekly, we had a test. It was often an open-book test. After the first three tests, I was failing miserably. I decided that I had to really apply myself to pass this course. On my own, I began to read the entire book, not just the assigned pages. When I took the next test, I got all the answers correct.

The ex-nun took me aside after class and asked me, "How and why did you cheat? I make up my tests so that no one should be able to answer everything correctly."

I was shocked. I responded, "I read the entire book, and I didn't cheat. Please get used to it because I am going to get As on all of your future tests."

And I did!

It was that class and that determination that prepared me for my interest in AIDS. When I graduated in 1979, AIDS had not yet surfaced as a disease. There were odd reports here and there, mostly on the two coasts, about unusual types of cancers and immune disturbances in a few gay men. By the mideighties, there was a name, AIDS, and a couple of target groups, gay men and drug addicts.

After coming out in the free and frenzied seventies, the horrible specter of AIDS arrived on the scene. In the beginning, there wasn't a lot of information about AIDS. Chiropractors were among the last health professionals to get educated about AIDS. I was sometimes asked to speak at the chiropractic college on the topic because I was one of only a few who had encountered actual patients who had AIDS. Gay men were coming to the hospitals with thrush, cancers, and healing disorders. They often lost weight, sometimes got dementia, often lost their eyesight to infections, and were unresponsive to the usual treatments. They usually died very quickly once the illness surfaced.

The Reagan administration chose to ignore the issue, maybe because it only seemed relevant for gay men and then later IV drug abusers. There were even those who thought it was a conspiracy to eliminate the more undesirable populations. For me, it was a terrible and depressing turnaround from the seventies, when gays were supposed to be proud and productive. Gay men and women dominated many career paths such as art, acting, music, and hairdressing. By 1985, AIDS had come to the Midwest with gusto, and because I was the first chiropractor to advertise in a gay paper in Minnesota, I started to get my first patients who had AIDS.

It was a challenge for me. I had some of my father instilled in me, and I was determined to show the world that chiropractic would be the ultimate cure for AIDS. I soon realized that the disease was progressing faster than anyone expected.

* * *

My first AIDS patient was a man in his early thirties. His parents called me for an appointment. When they and the patient came to my office, I was shocked. The son looked like an eighty-year-old man and one who was ready to be helped into a coffin. I wasn't prepared for the fragile and deteriorated structure that I was supposed to work on. I had to use the lightest touches, and even the muscle work had to be adapted toward very lean and toneless muscle tissue.

The parents' main concern was that their son smoked cigarettes. They were worried that he would fall asleep or die with a lit cigarette and burn the whole house down. They didn't want to deprive him of a few smokes because they were very aware that his days were numbered. I suggested that they keep the cigarettes themselves and only give them to him one by one to smoke at a time while they could be attentive. For them, that seemed too cumbersome.

It was one thing to have a stranger call on the phone to make an appointment. What was worse was when a friend or an acquaintance came in for a treatment and confided that they found out they tested positive for the HIV virus. All of a sudden, I found myself reading the obituaries in the newspaper every day.

My other concern was that often, the ones who tested positive were also the ones without cash flow or insurance. I wanted to be available for these guys without concern for money or contagion, but I even wondered how my other patients would feel if they knew that I was seeing AIDS patients in my office back-to-back with other patients. My ethics dictated that I keep the secret for myself and for my patients as much as possible. However, once a patient began their decline, their agonized physical appearance could hardly be camouflaged.

* * *

By '86, I had seen my first AIDS patient and also was told by a good friend, Bill, that he was diagnosed with AIDS while he danced for Joffrey in New York. Bill was the friend who introduced me to Fred, the Texan who I dated for a short time. Bill was a beautiful man, and I once thought that he would make a wonderful boyfriend for myself.

When he first told me about his diagnosis, he said, "I was diagnosed with AIDS in New York. The doctors there only give me six months to live."

I responded, "Not enough is known yet about AIDS. You need to pay strict attention to diet, exercise, rest, and supplements."

He went on to form his own dance company in Minneapolis. I went to one of his performances. He lived another couple of years and was physically active until his last several months. I even went to his wedding. Poor Bill was in the first line of trial-and-mostly-erroneous treatment for HIV. Eventually, in an effort to learn more about the disease, Bill underwent a spinal tap to find out if the virus was in the cerebrospinal fluids. It wasn't there, but the tap introduced a staph infection, which eventually killed Bill. He was a wonderful and talented man and a good friend of mine.

As the number of people who wanted help with HIV grew, I discovered Aliveness Project, which was just expanding into a new building. Steve, the director at the time, was open to any alternative or complementary methods of healing. I went over and talked to him, and he agreed to provide a space for me. I agreed to bring my grandmother's old horsehair-stuffed, leather-covered osteopathic adjusting table to the Project. Steve and the other volunteers signed people up, and I agreed to come twice a week after my regular practice to treat anyone who showed up. It was the best that I could do to try to help those with this disease, which was so misunderstood.

My passion to help was also my testament that chiropractic should be taken seriously as a drugless and effective intervention for most maladies. Many of my patients (understandable) and also most of my colleagues (inexcusable) feared that they would be endangering themselves and their uninfected contacts by merely touching an HIV-positive person. Everyone was so anxious about their own safety that they never considered that an HIV-infected person had a much better chance of getting sicker when in close contact with caregivers because of their immune system that was failing.

There was a lot of hysteria, especially in the beginning. Transmission modes were not well-known, and everything was suspect, even mosquito bites. I lost a few healthy but hysterical patients after they learned that I touched HIV-positive people. It was the new leprosy.

Chapter Seven

Buying My House

When Esther started coming to my office, it was my new home/office. It was situated on the lower level of my current house. For her, it wasn't that unusual for a chiropractor to work out of their house. Many chiropractors from the early twentieth century started and ended that way. She often walked the four blocks to my house, but when cold weather started in the early winter, she was able to talk various friends into giving her a ride.

* * *

I owned a small house about a mile away from Uptown in a nice neighborhood. I bought it in 1983 and dreamed for years about renovating it. The house had been a cottage at nearby Lake Calhoun. When Lakewood Cemetery expanded in the twenties, my house was moved to its current site, and an addition was added. Whoever moved it never put any footings underneath the house. It was placed on three layers of cinder block and left it that way for sixty years. I bought it from an estate of an old man and woman, who both died of cancer around the same time.

The house was very run-down. It was only about eight hundred square feet. It wasn't insulated. As a matter of fact, the west walls were two-by-fours on edge, making the hollow outer walls only two inches thick. When I moved in, I was afraid that there could be rats in the crawl space because there were large cracks in the block foundation. At the time, I was sharing two West Highland White

Terriers from an estranged partner, and I knew they were bred to be ratters. I always slept better when they were with me.

The house sat on a steep slope up from the sidewalk. It had an unusable tuck-under garage, which was built for early Model Ts. One had to climb several steps to gain access to the house. My dream was to dig away the steep bank on which the house stood and build a useable garage underneath the house. After living there a few years, I envisioned an office beside the old tuck-under garage and the incorporation of the existing garage into an office area. Then it would be much more accessible for patients.

My first winter in the house happened to be the snowiest winter on record for Minneapolis. I was struggling to make ends meet. I had no money for anything extra, and I spent much of my first winter there shoveling snow and waiting for warmer weather. I painted the ugly, smoke-permeated paneling that covered the plaster walls with bright, bold colors. A friend who visited once told me he felt as though he was in a Sunday cartoon strip. I finally bought a heater for my waterbed, and I kept the bed warm. I only heated the rest of the house to sixty degrees. Frost formed on the inside walls of my bedroom, and candles sometimes flickered out because of the migration of the cold air through the outside walls.

By spring of '84, I was really depressed. Most of the friends that I had known and associated with to this point had joined the Ronald Reagan political camp, and I felt as if a greedy free-for-all was taking place. I had a full-time cat that was part Siamese. Isadora was what I always had to come home to. While I tried to grow fond of her, my feelings for her were never the same as my feelings for my dogs.

Every other week, I also had the two dogs. I had to cordon off a part of the house for the cat. The dogs took over what remained. The cat could be on the dog side only if she straddled the curve of my neck as she lay across my shoulders.

One spring day, I was sick and tired of being sick and tired. I took a sledgehammer to a closet wall, and I started tearing out the entire interior of my house. Back in those days, the garbagemen would take anything. I set out the whole insides of my house in increments of two or three big black plastic bags each garbage day. I talked my electrician brother, Jim, into putting in all new wiring and worked out a payment schedule with him. I ordered several pieces of wallboard and delivered and moved them into the house on my own. I used the stack of wallboard as my dining room table for a few years. I also insulated all the walls and attic space and even took some R-30 rolls of insulation and wrapped the crawl space blocks from the inside.

Of course these improvements took several years to complete. Isadora was proficient in catching mice. At the time, I didn't know why I had so many mice, but when I discovered that there wasn't any foundation for my house, I understood how the mice could easily tunnel under the cinder block and become members of the household. That gave me another reason to put a garage under the house.

The beauty of my house was its location. It was on a parkway, and across the parkway was beautiful Lakewood Cemetery. When I first moved in, I saw wild turkeys, pheasants, foxes, and sometimes even deer in the cemetery. My house was the smallest one on the block. It had a big yard that was fenced in with chain-link. For me, it was affordable and allowed me to have the dogs, which wouldn't be possible in an apartment. I paid forty-three thousand dollars for it and had to jump through hoops to get financing, even with my retired father as a cosigner.

At the same time, I was putting in many hours at my uptown office, seeing patients. I liked my work as a chiropractor and enjoyed the artistic aspect of my work. I was good at assessing patients' conditions and skillful in relieving their pains. I learned a great deal from my father. He was exceptionally good at soft-tissue work, which I picked up on when I worked with him my first year out of school. What I never enjoyed was doing the paperwork necessary to be reimbursed by insurance. For me, a dyslexic, it was more difficult to use the appropriate medical terminology to describe my treatment than to translate English into French. No matter how hard I worked, it never seemed to be enough to bring the money that I needed into my life.

Chapter Eight

Uptown Office / Jerry

Esther first started coming to my office in November 1993. She often came more than once a week. It didn't take too long to establish a rapport with each other that was comfortable, caring, and mutual.

That was the year that I decided to incorporate massage therapy into my repertoire. I was excited about doing my own massage therapy. My receptionist, Louise, was also working for me then

*   *   *

I didn't know Esther when I had my office in Uptown. I started that in 1980 after my father asked me if I wanted to buy him out and work with my uncle Victor. Uncle Vic had eight children, six of whom eventually became chiropractors. Seeing the writing on the wall, I convinced my father to sell his half of the practice to Victor and lend me that money to start my own office in Uptown. The office rent there continued to increase every year, and I had to struggle to pay my bills.

My office was losing money, and I didn't have any visibility or parking options to offer patients. My landlord refused to allow me to put my name on a window of my second-floor office space.

My receptionist, Louise, was the mother of an early patient of mine when I was working in Uptown. She was twenty years older than I but seemed ageless. Louise had two children and had been divorced. One of the things I really liked about her was that she was interested in the world. It seemed like she always tried to make things better. She was a good counselor and helped me through a few rough times with relationship and family issues.

When Louise started working for me at my Uptown office, it wasn't a very difficult job. The job consisted of typing insurance forms and correspondences, answering phones, booking appointments, and helping to organize records. On my day off, I asked Louise to work a half day and clean the office. Her life was not her work. She studied massage and worked out of extra space that I had in my Uptown office. Louise also took some classes at the hospital on grief counseling. She was a cheerleader for me when times were tough and freely offered to me her down-to-earth acceptance of things.

Things got out of control after I took in two other chiropractors to try to make better use of the space I was leasing. One of them was obsessed with paperwork. The stack of paperwork he generated and passed on to Louise measured his personal self-esteem. Louise wasn't the fastest typist, and it added a huge amount of drudgery to her work. Louise also had some irritations with the female chiropractor. They didn't get along very well, and I think some of it had to do with the chiropractor's old issues surrounding her mother.

One of my associates even walked out the door with some of my patients and tried to coax them over to him. He eventually owed me a few thousand dollars, and he ended up declaring bankruptcy so that he could use the money he owed me for a down payment on his first house. I asked both associates to move out of the office after they said they couldn't pay what I determined to be their fair share. I knew that I couldn't do enough business to stay in that space.

All of this added to the tension in the office and ultimately led me to send away the two other chiropractors and leave Uptown in favor of my home. I was constantly inventing new and different ways to finance my life.

* * *

In 1983, I was driving my dad's old Buick station wagon. It cost about ten dollars for gas to drive to St. Paul back when gas was $1.20/gallon. That winter, '83–'84, was a horribly cold and brutal one. The previous summer, I met Jerry, who was a younger blond Nordic guy. He was an accountant. He was also a patient of mine, and it took a while before I could ethically suggest that we date. He had his own apartment. Jerry was neat and dressed very fashionably, sort of European. We went to a few dance performances and movies. We sometimes went out to eat. I developed a crush on him. Sex was compatible, and sleeping together was comforting.

I was lonesome at that time of my life. I visited my friend Miguel in New York City every year around Thanksgiving, and after my visit in 1982, I saw my first porno VHS tape on a big-screen television. When I came home from that trip, I immediately went out and charged a thirty-five-inch TV and a VHS player. It was such a great thing that I no longer had to go to bars to wonder if I was going to have a sexual encounter. I enjoyed having sex alone while watching it on TV.

Jerry was my first serious boyfriend since I broke up with Derrick. Jerry and I got along well together and had several mutual areas of enjoyment, but the winter of '83–'84 proved to be disastrous.

A few weeks before Christmas, Jerry confided in me and said, "My old boyfriend is going to be visiting from Amsterdam. He will be staying with me. For eight weeks, I don't want to see you, talk to you on the phone, or have any contact with you."

I was shocked. I thought we had something going, and now he wanted to deny my existence. I couldn't do anything about it.

The only bright spot in my life at that time was Jerry. Now the light was switched off. I got severely depressed. It was just before Christmas of 1983. I was driving the old bloated Buick station wagon that Dad gave to me. I was supposed to drive up to Mom and Dad's lake home for the holidays. It was bitterly cold and any travel out state was not recommended. I've hated Christmas ever since my parents overlooked me for gifts one year in 1962. I cried that night in 1962, and twenty years later, I cried driving alone up to the lake with only radio music to entertain me. I prayed that the car wouldn't break down because it was about fifty degrees below zero, including windchill.

Once at my parents' house, I couldn't even tell them why I was so sad. I saved my tears for when I was alone washing dishes or taking the dogs outside. The gifts were meager that year. I could barely afford anything for my parents. I splurged to buy a flourless chocolate cake for the Christmas feast. My youngest sister, Paula, was my only other sibling at the lake. On the drive back home, I made myself a resolution that I had to take charge of my life and stop wallowing in my misery. It's much easier said than done.

Business was usually slow around the two-week holiday period. Louise was there, and she was more joyful than I could ever be. Because of her background in grief ministry, I felt that I could confide my heartbreak to her. She was very supportive and was a big key to my recovery.

It got so bad, with so many sleepless nights. I would lie awake and would contemplate murder, double homicide, suicide, and much more. Several nights, I got into my frigid car, wielding a big butcher knife, and I would drive around and around the block stalking Jerry and his old boyfriend. Louise helped me get through those times and made me realize that no one was worth spending the rest of my life in prison for or, worse yet, ending my life.

The next thing I did was to get rid of my huge car. I drove it out to Burnsville. On the exit ramp to the car dealership, the car lost power, and I crept into the parking lot and found an empty spot. I test-drove a Nissan Sentra, brand new. Previously, I watched around me for several months to observe which cars were old and still running. Datsun (which became Nissan) won by a landslide. The salesman and I negotiated a price, and then I added that I had a trade-in.

We walked out to see the old Buick, and the guy asked, "Does this car actually work?"

I have trouble lying, so the only response I could give him with a straight face was, "Of course, how do you think I got here?"

He took the old car, and I drove away with a brand new Nissan. That cheered me up.

In early January 1984, I got an offer to look at a time-share at Breezy Point Resort. They offered a free computer just to show up.

Breezy Point wasn't too far from my parents' lake home. I decided that it would be impossible for me to buy a time-share after having just bought a new car. So I revisited my parents' lake home and made a side trip to Breezy Point. I was only thirty-three and not very wise, especially when it concerned sociopaths. I didn't realize that many time-share salespeople are sociopaths.

I was assigned a young handsome salesman, who said all the right things. "You deserve a vacation. You need to pamper yourself more. It's important to take a break from work sometimes." He even alluded to the possibility of inviting himself to share part of a week with me if I bought from him.

I left after buying week fifty, a blue week just before Christmas every year.

Anyway, the time-share was my only vacation for years to come, and at least I could drive to it in my new reliable Nissan. I got the new computer, but it was an early version of a computer that could only do basic mathematical calculations. I don't think the Internet even existed in 1984. By the time I had a new car and a new time-share and a new computer, Jerry's friend was leaving to go back to Amsterdam, and Jerry was finally ready to see me. I had already worked it out in my mind.

Jerry said to me, "My friend will probably come back again next year, and if I'm in a relationship, my friend will have to find another place to stay."

My last remark to Jerry was, "I thought we had a relationship, and since you are so addicted to your old friend, I no longer think it's a good idea to be friends."

Chapter Nine

Moving Gently Exercise

Even though Esther was elderly, she was still very active. However, right away, I noticed that when she walked, she waddled. Her weight shifted from one side over to the other in a rocking motion. She had a wide stance typical for older folks, who are well aware that falling is a leading cause of death in the elderly. She often asked me about my life, and I, in turn, asked about hers. After the first month of her visits, she readily gave up her cheap wig and handed it to me for safekeeping during her appointment.

I talked to Esther about an exercise program that I developed, which encouraged light movement for people, especially older folks. I gave her a book that I wrote, detailing the different exercises.

* * *

I started going to senior high-rises and giving gentle exercise classes in 1984. I developed a series of exercises, which incorporated a therapeutic and light movement activity set to old music of the Glenn Miller era. The premise I went by was to develop a program for myself that I'd be able to do my entire life, even if I lived to be 110. I spent two years making a video and writing a book detailing the exercises. It became a collaboration with a friend/patient, who was a videographer and an artist (my receptionist's son, who illustrated the book). I spent many hours in the editing booth and over ten thousand dollars of my own money (by way of VISA and MasterCard) and finished the first ever exercise video for grandparents. I hoped that it was my million-dollar idea.

On a fall trip to New York to visit Miguel in 1985, I went to Tower Records & Video in midtown Manhattan and talked with the manager of the store. She put my video on four or five public monitors in her store and played my video.

She liked it and said to me, "I will definitely order some copies for the Christmas season, but you have to first sell the video to my distributor. I can only buy from him."

I was on my way home to Minnesota; it was Friday and I couldn't stay until Monday to approach a distributor. I tried to call Monday, and the distributor wanted nothing to do with me. I didn't know anything about sales and marketing. The price for videos had fallen from $79.99 to $19.99 in the one-year period I was making mine. I got a business friend to try to help me, but she too struck out with the distributor. Later, I found out that even Richard Simmons had problems placing his exercise video for the disabled on store shelves.

Many of the people I used for the video were from the classes that I conducted at the senior high-rises. They were a great group, and I continued to go to two separate buildings once a week each and bring movement and music to the older women. Usually it was always women. Occasionally, a man would join us. My Saturday class always had a party after class, and everyone would contribute some snacks. Often the snacks would be from the free government rations of cheese and honey, with grapes or other fruit thrown in. The women sometimes told me stories about their lives, which I always found very interesting.

I call my work "Moving Gently Exercises." When people only watch the exercises, they come to the conclusion that the program isn't vigorous enough to do any good. I know from teaching it twice a week that it's excellent for all the muscles of the body and, when done a couple of times a week, prevents disuse atrophy, which is rampant especially in older populations. I feel it also strengthens bones as well as improves balance and confidence in the more frail folks.

Chapter Ten

Are You a Homosexual?

In 1987, I asked for help from Mom and Dad. As he had done a few times before, if I could convince him to help me, Dad would set up a loan with 4- or 5-percent interest. They sat at my dining room table. Actually, it was their old dining room table, which they gave to me some years earlier. My mother opened the conversation by saying that they both were concerned about my finances.

Then Dad took over and said, "We are more concerned about your eternal life because we think that you may be a homosexual."

Now it was never my intention to lie about my sexual orientation. I had a don't-ask, don't-tell policy long before Clinton. They knew for many years that I shared apartments with known homosexual men. I thought that they would accept me over time without my bringing it directly to their attention. So I was sort of taken aback when they sat there confronting me and suggesting that I would not be able to enter eternal life as a homosexual.

I answered that, indeed, I am gay and have been aware of it since I was five years old.

At that point, my mother burst into tears and said, "It's my fault. I shouldn't have encouraged you to cook and bake."

I answered, "It isn't anyone's fault. God made me this way for his purposes."

Then my father added, "If you don't change and start dating women, you will die from AIDS because that is God's punishment."

I countered, "If you believe that, you probably also believe that God gives diabetes to people as a punishment." My brother Dan had three kids, all of whom were type-1 diabetic.

Dad answered, "Yes, we do believe that disease is from God and has its purposes."

I said, "Dad, I am surprised that with your training as a doctor, you could think and say such things. I am disappointed that you believe such nonsense." And I added, "I know how one gets AIDS, and I also know how to avoid getting it." I continued, "I am more afraid that Paula will get AIDS when she drinks too much wine and finds herself in bed with a stranger." Paula is my youngest sister.

It was an odd conversation. One that usually takes place soon after coming out. Although I knew I was different by the age of five. When I was growing up, I thought it was unfair that only girls could wear colorful clothes of whimsical designs. Girls played fun games like jacks, jump rope, and dolls. Boys were always supposed to play power games, like cowboys and Indians, filling station, and physical games like baseball and football. I would rather play jacks, checkers, and chess. I didn't know exactly why I was different until I was nineteen. After the summer in Europe, I realized that while I enjoyed the company of women, my sexual desires were always for someone of my own sex. I preferred to embrace and kiss men rather than compete against them.

But growing up in a Missouri Synod Lutheran chiropractic family, I was taught that homosexuals were deviants who molested children. They were sick people. A chiropractor's family was never sick. Therefore, there couldn't be a homosexual in a chiropractic family. I was so confused growing up because all I wanted to do was to run around naked and look at other naked boys or men. When I saw my first Greek and Roman statues, I wondered why the women were always shown completely naked but men had fig leaves.

My parents decided to agree to help me with my business project. What I hoped to do was to make some improvements to the house I lived in so that I could begin a home/office business. I decided to build a room next to my tuck-under garage and dig under the main house and put a solid base in the form of a garage under it.

The added benefit would be a stable foundation. Mom and Dad said they were willing (despite the fact that I was now a confirmed homosexual) to lend me up to sixteen thousand dollars in order to do major construction. I thought this would be a good start, and I knew that I could do a lot of the work myself. So everyone agreed on that point.

On parting, my parents, who were now living at their lake home up north, added the last condition.

They said to me, "You are always welcome to visit us at our lake home, but please don't think of bringing any other homosexuals into our home."

My response to them was, "Okay, if that's what you want. I won't be visiting you either, so you'll have nothing to worry about."

With the loan from my parents, I was free to make a significant change in my life by first building my home office and subsequently reducing my overhead dramatically. I'd tried to see at least two patients at a time, going back and forth, and found out that I couldn't multitask effectively. I wanted to be able to concentrate totally on one patient at a time and devote all my attention to their problems. It wasn't going to work for me to do assembly-line chiropractic. Furthermore, the more time I gave to patients, the further away I got from doing the ten-minute shuffle. If I ever changed at this point, I would inevitably lose my regular patients.

One of my loyal patients was an architect, and he designed a workable remodel for my home office. It took me a full year to look into all the permits that I needed.

Chapter Eleven

Meeting Art

Esther was always a good conversationalist. She seemed interested in the world around her. I learned from her to ask people more about their lives. Esther wanted to know a lot about my life. While I am fairly open about my life to my patients, I am never quite certain how much I should divulge about myself.

As one of Esther's early questions, she asked, "Are you married?"

I responded, "No, I'm single."

Then she asked, "Have you ever been married?"

I answered, "No, I've never been married."

She continued to seek more information and asked, "What is it like living so close to work?"

I had to tell her, "I'm not living in my house upstairs."

Esther had been married twice. Her first husband died of heart problems. Her second husband died of cancer. She had an adopted son named Charles, who lived close by in a group home. He was in Viet Nam, and after combat, he was diagnosed as being paranoid schizophrenic. He was highly functional but didn't drive a car.

In the beginning, Esther came to my office a couple of times a week. Her main complaint was sinus drainage, which she claimed to have had since she was a little girl. Occasionally she also had headaches and some low back pain. Esther also suffered from arthritis, which was especially painful in her hands. At her age, it wasn't possible to make big corrections to her spinal joints and structure. A lot of what I did for her was soft-tissue work, which

I had learned from my father. I remember watching Dad "heal" strangers while on vacation just by touching them in therapeutic ways. I have to admit that he was very good with his hands and seemed to have a healer's touch. I only hoped that I could have the same effect on my patients.

I spend at least a half hour, sometimes forty-five minutes working with Esther. I ended the session with ultrasound, which was included with no fee to those over 65. I didn't take Medicare anymore but discounted my fees for 65-plus patients. It wasn't very long before Esther's curiosity started to expand. Since we bought lakeshore property in '91, I started going to the lake as many Minnesotans do in the summer. I explained to Esther that I went to my property in Northern Minnesota with my two Westies.

It didn't take long for her to ask, "Do you go there alone or with someone?"

I finally admitted, "I live with a good friend, Art, and I travel with him most of the time."

After that admission, from that point on, she always asked about how the dogs were and how Art was. Only she never got it into her head that my friend's name was Art. She always called him Harold. Harold was also the name of her second husband. Try as I may, I was never able to get her to call him anything other than Harold. So when she asked about Harold, I would transpose it and hear Art.

* * *

During the summer of 1987, I often went to Bare Ass Beach to get an all-over tan. This was a notorious beach on the Mississippi River, where I used to have lots of sex in the open air as well as tan nude in full sun. In the past, I'd sometimes have sex with four or five different men in an afternoon. While sex was sometimes still available there, I was more preoccupied with relaxation and solitude. With AIDS, the spontaneous and free sex was now a thing of the past, at least for me.

But one Wednesday, the third week of August 1987, I went to the beach before my senior exercise class. I was sitting in the sun when I looked over and noticed a handsome man about forty feet away from me. We were both enjoying the sun's warmth in our birthday suits, and soon, we were also looking and showing off a bit with each other.

Eventually, I went over and introduced myself. His name was Art. He was very friendly and seemed kind. He was attractive in a physical way but also very comfortable with his body, which I admired a lot. We played a little, very safely, and I found out that he had a boyfriend. I also had a boyfriend. When I had to go for my senior exercise class, Art helped me up the narrow footpath to my car, and I gave him my telephone number. I didn't expect him to call but hoped that maybe he would. At class that afternoon, I felt distracted, and my mind wandered to the distinguished man I'd met at the beach.

My boyfriend at that time was Fred. He was from Texas. Most of the people I ever met from Texas were a little different. Fred was a nice enough guy. He was transferred from Texas to work at Target. My friend Bill hooked us up on a blind date.

Fred was a few years younger than I. He was fastidiously clean and disliked almost all body hair. His hair was cut short, and he shaved most of the rest of his body. He was tall and Nordic, and he had a very nice butt. Fred was methodical in his approach to life and especially toward sex.

I was in a slow sexual mode myself, and because of the HIV epidemic, Fred was a comfort to have around. I lived at my house and Fred lived in his apartment. We were compatible in some ways, but he just didn't make my toes curl when we had sex. He was also uncomfortable because my dog was allowed inside and usually shared my bed.

Art was more interesting. He called a few times a week, and we would discuss the shortfalls of our respective boyfriends. Eventually, he asked if I wanted to come over to his apartment. I accepted his invitation. I was unprepared for the delightful time I had in his bed. We had a cocktail and we made love and sometimes smoked pot. Art smoked cigarettes. After I quit eight years earlier, I told myself that I wouldn't date anyone who smoked. But that seemed to be Art's only major fault. Sex with Fred was infrequent and predictable and usually followed a predetermined script. With Art, there was always a spontaneity and freshness that left me with my toes curled and my hair disheveled.

We began seeing each other a few times a week, and I looked forward to an invitation to snuggle. I didn't like to stay overnight. It became part of our routine that right after we had simultaneous and grand orgasms and before Art could smoke a cigarette, I would look at the clock.

Then I'd say, "Guess what? It's exactly 11:11 again."

It was so common for us to finish our wonderful sex at exactly 11:11 that we sometimes got the giggles whenever that time rolled around even when we weren't in bed. This seemed to be the exact moment for orgasm for at least the next five years.

When we didn't see each other, we talked on the phone. We often discussed our situations, and we realized how unhappy we were in our current relationships. Not only did Art have a boyfriend, but he also had a roommate. The roommate was purely an economic thing. One night, Art called and announced that he had broken it off with his boyfriend. Then he asked me when I was going to dump Fred. I was scared. I had never dumped anyone before. I liked Fred, but it was more and more obvious that Fred was never going to be my white knight. A friend of his visited from Texas and ended up flopping at his apartment for an unlimited stay. This friend wasn't gay, and Fred didn't want to be seen as gay around him. A final blow for me was when both Fred and his friend shaved their heads. This was a time when being a skinhead amounted to being a Nazi sympathizer. I was embarrassed to walk down the street with bald Fred.

I tried to tell Fred, "This relationship isn't working for me."

Fred listened and then said, "We can work things out. Maybe we'll have to change some things to keep our relationship."

I finally had to be blunt, and I told Fred, "I just don't want to be your boyfriend anymore."

It was a load off my chest, and I finally felt free to date Art and to invite Art into my house. I liked Art as a great friend. I was reluctant to say that I loved him. I loved his company and knew that he was an honest and caring guy. I wasn't sure how tangled up I wanted to get with Art, but I enjoyed his companionship and concerns. He was good to me and for me. I even tried to dissuade him from getting too serious by telling him some early parts of my sexual history. He remained persistent.

By the end of '87, Art told me that he was looking to buy a house. Art was a civil servant and had a good job with the state. Real estate was a good buy at the time. He eventually found the house of his dreams. The previous owner was a little old lady, who was going into a nursing home. Art was excited about becoming a homeowner. I didn't want to influence him in any way, so I stayed out of most of the process. My greatest concern for him was the location of the house.

The house itself was well built—stucco, one story with an expansion. It had a single-car small garage and a fairly large backyard. Art was anxious for me to see it, and it was a grand house. It had beautiful oak woodwork and a built-in oak hutch in the dining room. It was a type of Craftsman's house. It was on Second Avenue right next to the 35W Freeway on the east side. His friend Mark was going to live there as he had at the apartment.

* * *

Also that fall, I decided to get another Westie puppy. I located one in Fargo, North Dakota. Art and I drove to Fargo to bring the new puppy home. On the way back, I tried out names on the little girl, and when I said Nikki, the pup seemed to respond. So I named her Nikki Sioux to honor the Lakota Indians of the region. I had Eddie, my original male Westie, back at my house. He was already seven, and he'd been separated from his male sibling because of the breakup and the long-distance move of a former boyfriend, Derrick. Eddie took to Nikki really well, and he managed to potty train her single-handedly. They became quite a pair, and I always hoped to breed them some day.

Chapter Twelve

The Grand Remodel

By the end of 1993, Esther became a regular patient. She always came to see me at least once a week, sometimes twice. I was aware that she was lonesome and enjoyed getting out and coming to my office for a chat and bodywork. I had taken continuing education classes on geriatrics and knew the importance of being a good listener and conversationalist. Most chiropractors and medical doctors don't want to have to take the time with the elderly and don't give them a chance to ask questions. I have even heard that one downside of seeing older people was that they took too much time changing into gowns and dressing.

Esther knew that I was a patient man, and she was comfortable coming over to the office. In bad weather, she sometimes would get a ride from her cleaning lady or another friend. Just as she had with her husbands, Esther outlived all her drivers. She was always asking about my business, and she truly seemed to care that I was making a respectable living. I was always honest with her, and I told her truthfully if I was busy or not so much. I wasn't sure where she got her information about the world. It didn't seem like she watched much television, and I don't think she read the newspaper all that often. But she seemed to be abreast of most things that were happening in the world.

She complimented me on my office. When I told her that I had done all the work in the inside of the office, my talents surprised her. I explained to her how I'd changed my little house and showed her pictures of before and after. The before-and-after pictures showed an amazing difference.

* * *

After I had the plans drawn up for my new addition by my architect friend, I started planning the grand remodel. I wanted to start the project in the spring of 1989. My father was living up at the lake near Lincoln, Minnesota, and he had a small chiropractic office in the small cabin next door to the main house. He had a handful of patients that he worked on. It was through Dad that I found the James brothers. They were carpenters and bricklayers and builders in general and agreed to work on my remodel project. They were going to drive down Mondays from Motley, Minnesota, and live at my house during the week. Then they would leave Fridays to go back up north.

I had to get permits for all the construction. I went downtown to the permit office and filed for various permits. I needed one for excavation, plumbing, heating, electrical, water, sewer, and general construction. I talked to the guy who would approve the permits, and he took my architectural plans and said he would review them. Then I returned every Wednesday for six weeks to inquire on the progress. Every time, I talked to the same guy, and he always said he didn't have time to look over the plan. He quizzed me often.

He asked me, "Who drew the plans?"

I didn't want my friend to get into trouble, so I just said, "I drew them with the help of a friend."

He asked, "What kind of support would you use to put the steel beam on, the one which goes above the garage."

I answered, "Wood."

He corrected me and said, "It has to be a cement-block support."

He was making me crazy, and on the fifth visit, I told him, "I've had enough. I want you to do your job already. I have a bobcat and dump truck reserved, and I am going to start excavating in two weeks with or without a permit."

He stopped toying with me and said to me, "I won't give you the permits until you have a structural engineer sign off on all the weight-bearing loads. I am also going to visit the site myself to make sure the project is feasible."

Part of the deception that I had to entertain was the fact that legally, I couldn't add an office to my house. It had to be presented as a rec room and an extra bedroom.

When the bureaucrat got to my house, he asked me, "Why do you want more space on the lower level?"

I introduced him to Eddie and Nikki, my Westies, and said, "I want more room for the dogs."

I also happened to know a structural engineer, who agreed to sign off on the plan.

I finally got the permits and started planning for the excavation. I found a rental company that had a dump truck and a bobcat for rent. I reserved them for a weekend and planned an excavation party. I was going to make a Brazilian stew, which included beef tongue and black beans. I made stew and salad for a small crew. I was naive enough to think that we could excavate all the dirt in front of the house in one weekend. I even found a place to dump the fill for free a couple of miles away on the other side of Lake Calhoun, where houses were being destabilized from sinking ground.

I was geared up to learn to drive a bobcat for the first time, and Art was going to drive the dump truck. That Friday, I got a call from the rental company, and I was told that the people who still had the rented bobcat needed it one more day. I couldn't get it until Sunday. I had five people lined up to help and had made the Brazilian stew. I cancelled the party. Art and I picked up the bobcat and dump truck as early as possible Sunday morning. We started digging and dumping, but it was slow at first because neither of us had ever done this before. At one point, I knocked Art off the truck with an errant push on the controls of the bobcat. Fortunately, he wasn't seriously injured. By nightfall, we only had three loads of dirt out of the hill, and our progress was barely noticeable.

Monday morning, the James brothers showed up. They both said together, "We thought you would have all the excavation finished when we showed up."

I told them, "I got the bobcat late, and it took longer than I thought it would. Can you guys finish the digging?"

They said, "Yah, I guess we can finish digging."

The dirt that we moved was more dirt than the sinking houses wanted. I needed to find another place to dump clean fill. I finally found that Hedberg Aggregates would take the rest of it, and we needed to pick up gravel and sand from them anyway.

The following weeks, the James brothers brought their own dump truck that had to be rolling in neutral in order to pop the clutch and a homemade bobcat made of spare tractor parts. I went to my Uptown office in the morning and drove one or two loads of dirt to Hedberg at lunch and went back to work later in the day. I would pick up cement or gravel or sand and bring it back. Once, I made the mistake of turning off the engine of the dump truck at Hedberg. I couldn't get it to start. No one had cell phones back then. I finally had to have one of the guys at Hedberg push the dump truck so that I could jump start it.

When I was building my home office, Louise marveled at my skillful use of credit cards to accomplish my goals. I took out several cards at the same time so that one company didn't know what the other was thinking. Then I played credit card roulette to purchase materials for my building process. In the end, I had my house reappraised for a much higher value. I finally took out a new loan on my own, dropping my father as a cosigner on my mortgage. Then I used the new value of the house and loan to pay off the credit card balances.

The whole project was supposed to take two months and cost sixteen thousand dollars, which my father had agreed to lend me. Banks would only laugh at me if I'd tried to get a loan through them. The project actually cost over sixty thousand dollars and wasn't completed until after six months. It was a big job. We cut down the entire hill that my house stood on. Then we dug under the house while it was up on telephone posts used as stilts. Once the dirt was gone, we saw that the joists under the floor of the house were only two-by-fours every twenty inches. We had to replace them all with two-by-eights every sixteen inches.

The foundations were poured and the blocks were laid. Eventually, we set the house back down on the new foundation. I found decorative blocks for the visible part where the office was going to be. I ordered new triple-pane windows and the doors for both outside and inside. One weekend, I was told to rent a hammer drill and cut into the old garage cinder-block wall. I wasn't sure what that tool was, but I rented it and cut out an eight-by-six-foot and three-by-six-foot section of the old block wall. I worked so late into the night Sunday that Art came over to see if I was all right and to make sure the cement ceiling hadn't fallen in on me.

We had to move the gas line, and the waterline had to be dug in deeper. During all this time, my house was completely open, and I sometimes had the neighborhood cats running through the house trying to catch mice. Mice were making holes in the walls upstairs and breeding. The two bicycles that were in the open garage were stolen. Their loss wasn't noticed for over a month because of the chaos of construction.

Fortunately, 1989 was a drought year. Lack of rain allowed us to dig in the sandy soil without having too much washout. Once, I came over to the house to see the progress and noticed that the dirt along the back wall of the new garage was beginning to cave in. The shallow footings of the neighbor's six-foot wooden fence were showing. I had to quickly slather a tar sealer on the new cinder block and backfill the wall by hand as fast as I could. The neighbors were not very happy with the whole process, but I managed to save their fence and prevent a catastrophe.

Sometimes, even my father came to help. He was seventy years old and came to work in his old work clothes. He often brought me cans of old used and bent nails.

I told him, "Dad, a box of new good nails cost less than four bucks."

His reply was, "Then I just saved you four bucks!"

Because the nails were old and rusted, it usually took too much time to try to use them, and I discarded them when Dad wasn't looking. He worked really hard, and it was in the hot weather of July and August. I tried to assign him easy tasks that weren't overwhelming, but he seemed to thrive on hard work.

Art also helped a lot, and he frequently came by to rescue me from the night. He owned an old Ford Taurus, which we often took with a trailer hitched to it to get supplies at the building supply stores. There weren't any stores open twenty-four hours then, and we usually pulled into the yard of the stores ten minutes before they close. We knew where almost everything was and knew it better than most of the employees. I used one of my many credit cards. I rotated them as they became full. I started living at Art's house all the time, and when he wasn't right there helping, he was usually making supper for me.

Near the middle of the project, money was running out. The James brothers had an argument and drove back and forth separately. Art joked that the three-month project would probably not be done by the time of the State Fair (early September). His perception was right on the money. By Labor Day, I moved out of my Uptown office and into the new home space. Things were not completed, but the office area was finished enough to receive patients. My receptionist, Louise, helped me get things set up as best we could, and there were a lot of stuff that we just tossed into the new garage and the back room.

It was a small space without much storage and much smaller than we were used to. But there was a sense of newness, and the space was bright and cheerful. The new carpet had the aromas of chemicals, which some green reviewers deemed poisonous. The driveway wasn't paved yet, and the sidewalk and curbing were not finished. My first few patients seemed to feel that it was a good move. At least they didn't have to worry about parking. It was a big accomplishment, and it would save me a lot of overhead money starting almost at once.

Chapter Thirteen

The Lake Property

Esther usually was able to get rides to my office during the long Minnesota winters. She had grown up on a farm in Shakopee, Minnesota. Esther had several siblings. I believe she was the third girl out of four girls and two younger boys. She sometimes talked about how she and her sisters churned butter on the front porch. She had a favorite brother named Calvin after Calvin Coolidge. He worked for Boeing in Seattle. Of course in 1993, he was retired. He was a big engineer for them, and he spent a year in Germany after World War II.

Working on Esther the very first time, I noticed that she was missing the tip of her left index finger. I didn't mention it until sometime later.

I finally asked, "What happened to your finger?"

She told me, "My older sister slammed the Model T car door while my finger was in the door frame. It was mangled and it had to be removed."

She had been missing it for most of her life.

* * *

Since 1991, Art and I started going up to the lake on weekends. We bought our land on a lake up north in 1991. We'd been looking around for lake property for a while and went to a late winter Home & Garden Show one weekend. One of the realtors at the show was featuring a lot on Loon Lake in Otter Tail County. A married couple just ahead of us was scheduling an appointment to look at it the following weekend. When it was our turn, Art and I decided to look at the lot Wednesday before the other couple.

It was March, and there was still quite a bit of snow on the property. Thick ice covered the lake. We looked at the property with the realtor, and then she left, and Art and I talked about it together. I had an odd sensation of tranquility and spirituality while at the land. Art was more conservative, and he felt we shouldn't buy the first thing that we looked at. I reminded him that we looked at a couple of other properties just driving by them before, so this wasn't the first one. This land seemed different to me. We finally decided to buy it, and we went back to Alexandria to fill in the paperwork.

Once we had land, we decided to make the most of it. We went up to the land almost every weekend from June to September. We built a three-section dock in Minneapolis and used my dad's boat trailer to haul it up to the lake. On the way up there with the dock, the tilt mechanism of the trailer came undone, and we dropped our load all over Interstate 94 just past St Cloud. Thank God we were not injured, and no one was killed. I secured the load once again, but we drove the rest of the trip watching to make sure that it didn't happen a second time.

We soon got discouraged packing everything we needed each time that we traveled the two hundred miles up north. We agreed to build a storage shed and decided that we'd put an outhouse in one corner of it. Late July, early August of '91, we planned a whole week up at the lake, and we prepared to build an eight-by-twelve-foot shed. There wasn't any power or water up at the lake, so I designed the shed and cut many of the pieces of wood with a power saw at home in Minneapolis.

Once we arrived with a trailer full of stuff, we put up the tent and screen tent and unpacked our camping gear. Then we began to dig a deep outhouse hole. The dirt was sandy and prone to cave-ins. We also had to flatten an area to place the four-by-fours that would be used for the foundation. The week we chose to do the work was exceptionally warm. Our lot didn't have trees on it except near the lake. We tried to do the hardest work during the early mornings and late evenings. When we got too hot during the daylight hours, we would strip naked and run and jump into the lake to cool down. We didn't have neighbors, so it was easy to skinny-dip and run around free of clothes.

We didn't sleep well because even the nights were hot and muggy. We were in our tent, in sleeping bags that were open. There was a four-inch-thick foam pad that we put the sleeping bags over. The dogs slept in the tent with us. Back then, it was Eddie and Nikki.

One night, I had a vision. It was like a dream except that it made sense, and I still remember all the details. It happened the night after I found a bone while digging. This was a bone about five inches long and three inches wide and had a rough carving of a deer on it. When I showed it to Art, he laughed.

He said, "How did you carve the deer on the bone so fast?"

I told him, "I didn't. That's how I found it."

That night, an Indian chief came to me in a vision and told me that the land we bought was sacred land. Many years ago, Indians used the area to pull their canoes up on shore and scout from on top of the prairie hill. The women collected berries and asparagus from the area, and the men hunted deer and sometimes buffalo.

Indeed there are still wild raspberries, strawberries, and asparagus growing on our land. The area is a natural amphitheater, and sound collects in the area that our land occupied. A few years later, we noticed that we could pick up television signals on a small battery TV with only the small built-in antenna. When the Empire Express train passes and blows its horn several miles away at two in the morning, one would think we were sleeping on the tracks.

The chief told me exactly how we could attach the roof to our shed. I had been wondering how to do it. Then he went on about three people in my life that I was having conflicts with. He talked to me about each one, one at a time. He told me how to handle each situation. I woke up somewhat in disbelief. We attached the roof, and it held perfectly just as the Indian told me it would. I told Art about the vision, and he mentioned that there were some mounds around the property. I noticed them but thought they were big anthills. It also reaffirmed to me that the land was sacred.

The chief ended the conversation with me by saying that he was confident about my stewardship of the land. I pledged to plant an orchard around the mounds. I was never afraid at night up there, even though one night a bear walked within inches of our tent. It was feeding on the wild raspberries. The next morning, I discovered bear droppings. I had heard the bear groan while walking by.

I asked Art, "Do raccoons make grunting sounds?"

He answered, "No, but bears do."

Thank God the dogs were tired out and didn't hear the bear. I am sure that, as city dogs, they wouldn't have been matched well to go against a wild bear.

We had many fun times up at the lake lot. In 1992, we planted 150 baby trees and went up to water them each weekend. We'd haul water from the lake in five-gallon buckets. We lost less than 10 percent of them, even though it was a drought year. The weekend we planted them was Mother's Day weekend. Our plan was to spend the night in a motel because it was still cool at night, and we had the two dogs. We planted from the time we arrived until just before dark. We arrived at the motel in Detroit Lakes and registered. We told the management that we had one dog. Since our dogs looked identical to most people, I took them out one at a time. They'd played in the prairie grass all day, and when we laid down for sleep, wood ticks started climbing off the dogs by the hundreds. I didn't know this at the time, but wood ticks can only climb up. They have to drop or jump down.

All night long, the ticks would climb up, and they eventually were climbing on Art and me. I turned on the light, and I was able to kill them by cutting them in half with my fingernails. Art just flicked them away to let them start their climbs all over again. By morning, I'd hardly slept, and I looked at the clock. I thought the clock said 9:30 AM. I took each dog out separately. The second time, I got locked out. I had to wake Art to get the second dog back in.

Art asked, "What time is it?"

I told him, "It's nine thirty."

He got up and went to the bathroom and was in the shower. When I checked the clock again, I realized that I'd read the big and little hands wrong. It was really only 5:45 AM. I expected Art to murder me when he found out. Then I looked up at the ceiling. During the night, most of the wood ticks had climbed all the way up there. I'm not sure why they weren't on us, sucking blood. Dozens of them were coating the ceiling. We left to get breakfast. Neither of us had gotten the sleep we needed, but we got all the trees planted and returned home safely.

Once the shed was built, we no longer had to pack everything that we would need each weekend. We could store the tent, sleeping bags, grill, and camp stove up there, along with the sledgehammer and stuff for the boat. We had a picnic table from Art's mother's lake cabin. We also got a small aluminum fishing boat from her. The first few years at the lake were full of adventure.

We decided to paint the shed a few weeks after we built it. Our lot was at the end of a cul-de-sac. So we both took a gallon of paint and a brush and started on opposite sides. It was a hot day in August and not long after we started, I stripped down naked so I wouldn't get paint on my clothes. I didn't say anything to Art, who was around the corner. When he turned the corner, we looked at each other and giggled. He was naked too! Then within just a few minutes, we heard a car approaching on the little-used gravel road. We only had enough time to get our shorts on before it came to a stop in the cul-de-sac. I have no idea why the people chose to drive down the gravel road, but it almost seemed as if the lake and woods had eyes and ears. .

Another time, we got up to the lake early on a Saturday afternoon and proceeded to set up camp. The sun was blazing. We put up the sleeping tent after mowing the grass and took a break. I was feeling weak. We finished putting up the screen tent over the picnic table. We turned on the portable radio and then got naked and ran to the lake to cool down with a swim. The dogs loved to swim too. The water felt good and, as usual, made me a little frisky. We went back to the screen tent. Before very long, we were playing with each other on the picnic table. We just finished our climactic orgasms when an announcement blared from the radio. No, it wasn't 11:11, but it had just hit one hundred degrees in downtown Fargo. We laughed and then noticed a young man bass fishing near enough to have observed the entire performance.

The lake served the purpose for us to leave the city and travel. It was a long drive, three and a half hours, but it was as if we were on another planet when we were there. Art and I enjoyed travel, and we had to keep things on a budget, so the lake was a good investment.

Chapter Fourteen

Palm Springs—AIDS Connection

Esther always asked about Eddie and Nikki and "Harold" each time she entered my office. The spring of '94, Art and I went on a trip to Palm Springs again. When I came back, Esther asked me about the trip. It was one part of my life that I didn't think I could fully share with Esther.

* * *

We've been going to Palm Springs since at least 1991. Sometimes we went twice a year. We've been there many different times of the year. Our first trip was a unique adventure. One of my patients/ friends came to see me regularly after he found out he was HIV positive. Aaron was a tall, dark, and handsome man, who graduated from a small college in Iowa with a major in music. He had a life partner, Victor. I got to know both of them as friends. Aaron was not faring well with his HIV treatment. He was one of a few people who came to my office rather than get treatment at Aliveness Project, where I volunteered. He had diarrhea, nausea, wasting, and, toward the end, he developed rashes and skin sores.

Aaron didn't have a lot of money, but he needed a lot of treatment. After a few sessions, I told him to make it a point to come and see me once or twice a week for no charge. He did this. I did all I could to help him live a life of quality. He paid me once in a while, sometimes in kind. Once, the four of us went to a Twin's baseball game at the old domed stadium. That was quite the comedy. Four gay men watching baseball in the nosebleed section at The Dome, with only rudimentary knowledge of the game and very little interest in keeping score. After about the fourth inning, we wandered the outer hallways. A woman approached us and offered us admittance tickets to the Elite Club Room. She assured us that we could get cocktails and sit and talk. We took her up on that, and we found the room. We had a few cocktails and talked about everything besides sports. The game ended, and we were still talking as people filed out past the small windows. We didn't even know who was playing against the Twins or who won, but we had a good conversation with each other.

Aaron was pretty sick for about a year and a half. Not before long, Victor asked if I could come to their apartment rather than try to bring him to my office. It's harder for me to give a good treatment at a home, but I obliged him. Aaron always said that he was going to put me in his will. My only response was that we could cross that bridge when we got there. Before he died, Aaron put on a one-man music show. There were many radical fairies there, and there were a lot of "Silence = Death" posters. Aaron died a few months after his show.

I stopped attending most HIV funerals after my good friend Bill died. Victor came to my office about six weeks later and presented me with a check for two thousand dollars. He gave me the check, and he told me Aaron wanted me to have a part of his life insurance settlement. I was touched. I didn't really expect that much money.

When I told Art about it, I said, "Aaron wouldn't want me to spend the money on bills." Aaron was a proud man, and he always wanted to tell the world that it was perfectly acceptable to be a gay man.

I asked Art, "Would you be interested in using the money to go on a trip?"

We both decided that we should try out Palm Springs, California. We had seen ads in the gay newspaper about several gay, clothing-optional resorts. The thought of running around naked in the warm sun appealed to both of us.

So I called several resorts and got a few brochures. We decided on the resort whose pamphlet showed the most nudity and which also had nice rooms. Then we planned the rest of the trip. To save some money, we chose to fly into Las Vegas, stay overnight, rent a car, and drive through the San Bernardino Mountains and on to Palm Springs. We were excited about the trip, and we started packing days before we finally boarded the plane. The night before, I rented an X-rated video, and we watched *Love Gods of Las Vegas*.

I joked to Art and said, "We might see some of these guys from the movie in Palm Springs."

We got into Las Vegas late, after midnight. We took a room at Circus Circus. I couldn't stand it. The room had bold-colored, striped wallpaper, and of course, it had no clocks. We tried to get some food, and at 1:30 AM, nothing seemed to be open. We had to settle for a sandwich and fries. We tried to sleep. At 6:00 AM, I was dressed and ready to get out of Vegas. We found an all-you-can-eat buffet that served cheap, barely edible food. Then we drove and drove. This was our first time driving through a desert. When we got to the top of the San Bernardino Mountains and started descending, we both screamed, and I held tight to the steering wheel. It was as if we were on an out-of-control roller coaster. I glanced at the speedometer and saw it register over 100 mph. I cautiously braked, and we slowed to 80 mph. We got to Palm Springs in about four hours. It should take closer to six. We found the resort, and we were greeted by one of the owners. As we were led through the gate, I poked Art and pointed to the guy near the hot tub. It was one of the stars of *Love Gods of Las Vegas*, totally nude, doing some promo pictures.

We both laughed. John showed us to our room, and then he started making sexual advances, which ended in a three-way orgy. John left and we started to unpack. There were naked men by the pool, and we could see them from our window. We didn't know what the protocol called for. Does one walk out stark naked right to the pool and sit down on a towel brought from the room? Do you wear a bathing suit to the pool and then take it off?

Art said, "You go first."

I answered, "No, you go first."

Finally, I went first, and Art followed after me, both of us completely naked.

It was a nice resort. At that time, there were only seven rooms. The other guys who were staying there were friendly and sociable. This was the resort that we stayed at for our Palm Springs trips for the next four years. When I talked to Esther about these trips, I only mentioned that we liked to relax at the pool and have cocktails. That's when she mentioned to me that her first husband drank too much.

An Early Midlife Crisis

Chapter Fifteen

Mom's Health / My Career Doubt

When Esther first came to see me in 1993, I had just made some big decisions about my life. My mother died from cancer after an eight-month struggle. I'll never know if earlier intervention would have saved her. A part of me blamed my father for not getting medical attention until it was too late. He did the same thing five years earlier when we found out my mother had diabetes.

* * *

I'd just had the conversation with my parents about HIV being a punishment from God, and I countered that then they must believe diabetes was also God's punishment. That was in 1987. They told me that yes, it really was their belief. Unfortunately, Mom got sick only a month later.

They lived at their lake home, which I'd told them I would never visit. I called on the telephone at least once a week. I called for several weeks in November '87, and Dad answered. Each time, he told me Mom was in bed and couldn't come to the phone. At first I didn't think too much about it. After a couple of weeks and with Mom still in bed, I asked my father what he thought was wrong.

He answered, "She either has a bad flu or she might be diabetic."

This disturbed me, that there was a chance that she was diabetic, and he wouldn't do anything to confirm it. I hung up and tried to figure out how to get my father to do the right thing.

I called back the next day, which was a Sunday. Dad was surprised that I called again so soon. Mom wasn't doing very well at all. She was very weak and couldn't eat anything.

I told Dad, "Put Mom on the other phone in the bedroom."

When I heard her, she could barely speak. I told Dad, "Monday, you are going to get Mom out of bed and take her to see a medical doctor. He will have some blood tests run for diabetes."

Dad reiterated, "Dave, you know that we don't believe in medical doctors."

I said, "It doesn't involve a belief system to get test readings for a blood screening." Then I asked, "Mom, do you understand all of this?"

She said, "Yes, I understand."

I told Dad, "You are obligated to do this." And I told them both, "Spend some time and find a clinic nearby tonight and call first thing in the morning to set it up."

That was about all that I could do. I wondered why none of my five siblings was willing to light a fire under Dad.

The next day, Monday, Dad took Mom to an osteopath to have her condition assessed. Thank God the osteopath was smart enough to do the right tests well. He advised my father to admit Mom to the Brainerd Hospital because she was nearly in a coma. She was in the hospital for several days and had severe neuropathy in the legs and feet from that point on for the rest of her life. My father somehow gave me all the credit for willing Mom to get diabetes. I don't know why he thought I possessed that much power.

* * *

When Mom was in Rochester with cancer in 1993, we three boys and sister Paula went with the spouses to visit her. While in the cancer ward, I spied Mom's chart on her door and started to read it. A short while later, a nurse came and ripped it from my grasp and told me that I wasn't allowed to read it. I told her I was a son and a doctor, but she was determined to keep the chart out of my hands. I'd read enough to see that Mom had stage-IV cancer and that it'd spread into her abdomen. It was breast cancer but never manifested in the breast itself. It was terminal, but I didn't get to any part where they said how long it might be. I told the others after we stopped at a restaurant along the return route. Nearly everyone was in a state of denial and didn't want to believe me.

Mom struggled with cancer through that summer. Even though she was in advanced stages of breast cancer, my father allowed her to choose chemotherapy as a hopeful treatment. It took a tremendous toll on her. She had all the horrible side effects that were to be expected. Nausea, hair loss, weakness, and fatigue were all part of her day. When she was feeling better, she unilaterally lifted the lake-home ban imposed on me because of my homosexuality. My mother asked me to come and visit her and to bring Art along with me. We sometimes stopped there on our way up to our own lake property. Once, Art brought his renowned beef Stroganoff. It was one of the few meals that Mom raved about and had an easy time eating.

There was a surreal atmosphere at their lake home. It never occurred to me that Dad really didn't know how to cook. He was pretty good at giving Mom live-in, day-to-day maintenance. It wasn't acceptable to talk about Mom's progress or deterioration. My sister Paula sometimes spent time helping Dad. I called and chatted often with Mom. I asked her, when she had the strength, if she'd organize some of her favorite recipes. I eventually made a cookbook for my siblings and myself. Some of the recipes were written in her own handwriting.

A gay man's relationship with his mother is one of the most important female relationships that he will ever have. I loved my mother dearly, and I felt that she would sacrifice everything to benefit her children. When I received the news that she died, even though it was expected, it was emotionally traumatic. I always thought it would've been better for me to lose my father first. There was more than a little anger in me toward him, over the delays in Mom's treatment.

The days before the funeral, I experienced waves of sadness and periods of tears. Art was always there to comfort me. I remembered all the beautiful flowers at the mortuary and church. Mom used to be the principal person in charge of flower arrangements at her church for many years. One thing that stood out for me at the funeral was the makeup on Mom in the open casket. When the family was given a preview, I gasped when I looked at Mom lying in the wooden coffin. They put bushy Brezhnev eyebrows on her emaciated face, which looked like a skeleton. She had only a tiny hook left as a nose. I felt that either something should be done to the eyebrows or the casket should be closed. The eyebrows were tweaked, but I thought the overall final appearance was dreadful.

Later that fall, Dad called me and told me that I should come up to their lake home to help sort Mom's things. The rest of my siblings had already been there and had asked about items that they wanted to have for their memories. When I got there on a Saturday afternoon, it was just Dad and I. Things were strained because we were both in our own worlds of grief, but they were such different worlds. I asked about the rocking chair that I cherished from my youth. My father said I could have that. Everything else that I asked about was previously assigned to another sibling. Finally, I saw the small art deco table lamp that I always thought was beautiful. Dad told me that he thought he wanted it for himself. So I said good-bye and left after only a few hours.

A couple of weeks later, Dad stopped at Art's and my house with a large box of junk. It was mostly old cleaning solutions and potting soils. When I invited him in, he was gushing with news that an antique dealer from Brainerd stopped by the lake house and offered him one hundred dollars for the art deco table lamp that I'd wanted. He readily sold it. I was so angry with him that I was speechless. After Dad left, I tossed everything that he brought me into the trash.

* * *

All the family craziness, Mom's illnesses, and Dad's reluctance to accept me as a gay son made me think I'd made the wrong choice about being a chiropractor. To make matters worse, insurance coverage for chiropractic care was in its infancy. There were several different companies all with different pay schedules and different forms to file with different plans and deductibles. Several of the big insurance companies required participation—in the form of a contract. The whole setup was nearly impossible to navigate through by a single doctor / one-staff office. I sometimes had to submit the same form three or four times before it would finally be accepted or rejected. Early in 1993, amidst the angst of a dying mother, Blue Cross Blue Shield told me finally that a claim for $250 would not be paid because I hadn't jumped through the hoops in the proper order. They further stated that the patient couldn't be billed either because it wasn't their fault. How can anyone run a business without having any idea if they'll ever get paid or how much they'll get paid? I hated my failures and even thought about my brother's comment about God and my lifestyle. I was very unhappy.

I began to wonder what else I could do with my life. Art and I had been going to Palm Springs since about 1991 at least once a year. There were several gay, clothing- optional men's resorts there, and it occurred to me that maybe this was something that could succeed in Northern Minnesota on a secluded lake. I began doing research on that subject. I even went so far as to visit two different resorts in Northern Minnesota, which were for sale. I wanted to offer massage and spa-type services as well as outdoor swimming, hiking, and skiing. I even envisioned sleigh rides in the winter with naked men wrapped in furs. But after a lengthy process, I realized that most gay men in the Twin Cities were not going so far as Northern Minnesota to take a break. Men in other parts of the country weren't going to fly to Fargo when they could go to Fort Lauderdale.

I liked the idea of doing massage and always thought that it was a good combination with chiropractic alignment. I hated trying to get paid from insurance companies. All other aspects of my work were satisfying. I decided in 1993, after my mother died, to drop insurance and to begin offering massage therapy at my home office. This decision was made just before Esther began coming to my office in the fall of '93.

One of Mom's dying wishes was for brother Dan and I to reconcile. I made an effort to meet Dan for lunch. He lived in

Buffalo and invited me out for lunch. Before the meeting was fixed, he called and asked if he could make spaghetti at his home, and I agreed to that. I pulled up to his house on Lake Pulaski and found him in the last three-car garage (out of two of them) covertly smoking a cigarette just as a delinquent teenager might do. He was also having insurance reimbursement problems for his chiropractic office. I told him that I was considering opening a gay resort.

He looked at me and asked, "What on earth is a gay resort?"

I told him, "It is a resort for gay men."

All he did was to shake his head. The spaghetti was an odd assortment of different pastas with processed tomato sauce and some pregrated cheese. I left knowing that I'd tried but wondering why I bothered to get closer to Dan.

By the time I saw Esther for the first time, I was already studying massage therapy. My receptionist, Louise, helped me put things together systematically. Louise had taken classes from Sister Roselyn and had given massages in my office at Uptown. She was quite good. I also found a video made by Sherri Bellefonte on how to give a massage. Of course, I knew how to do a lot of soft-tissue work as a chiropractor, and I'd taken acupuncture and studied acupressure. I traded in one of my two hi-lo chiropractic adjusting tables for a flat table, the height of which could be adjusted by an internal elevator. I bought sets of sheets and got together an assortment of lotions. I practiced on Art a lot, but it often turned into a sexual thing when I was at home. I am sure Art thought that's what would happen in the office too.

* * *

After Dad told me he sold the table lamp, I talked to Art about my feelings. Art suggested that I sleuth around and find out the name of the woman Dad sold the lamp to. In a phone conversation, Dad told me the woman's name. I was able to track her down. I called her and told her that the lamp had a special meaning to me. I knew what she paid for it, and I wanted to buy it back for $150.

She agreed to sell it back to me. Art was actually going that way on a road trip for work, so he bought back the lamp for me.

When Dad came over that Christmas, he was surprised that I had a lamp so similar to Mom's on the mantle.

He asked, "Where did you find another lamp like that? It looks exactly like the one I sold to the antique dealer."

I told him, "It's the same lamp. I found the woman that you sold it to and bought it back from her. I told you that I wanted the lamp."

I hoped he finally understood how I felt about it.

Chapter Sixteen

Breezy Point

Breezy Point was my winter time-share vacation, which I used for many years. Most of the time, I only spent three or four days of my week there. It was a winter week, and I enjoyed cross-country skiing and catching up on movie videos. The first time I went up there, I'd forgotten the kitchen layout. I brought a sixteen-pound frozen turkey and groceries to make Christmas cookies and my Christmas cards and address book. Once there, I had to laugh. There was no oven, only a microwave. There were a couple of electric burners and a refrigerator and a trash compactor. I cooked the turkey in the microwave, but first, I had to thaw it and then cut it into pieces. It still took several hours. I was fascinated with the trash compactor. I loved to put empty glass wine bottles in it and listen to the glass shatter. I thought it was one of the dumbest inventions ever made. But it was really fun to play with.

In the early years, there was usually plenty of snow for my week. Ten years later, there was no guarantee that there'd be any snow or even ice on the lake. Art started going up there with me after we met. After the first time, he chided me about not using the ice-fishing houses that could be checked out at the front desk and were free to owners. That second year, we went to Brainerd to buy poles and gear for ice fishing, and we tried to catch fish.

It was a novel thing for me. I didn't understand how the fish were going to be waiting right under the house so they could be caught. Our first time out, the office told us that the house we signed up for had a bad heater, and we weren't allowed to change the controls.

We drove out to the house in the midafternoon. We ducked into the house. I'm not sure why they couldn't build the houses just another six inches taller. There were two metal card-table chairs, the heater with a sign (DO NOT TOUCH THE CONTROLS), and of course, the two holes through the ice to catch fish. It was fairly cold outside but very warm inside. We had a beer and I immediately got bored. I tried to play a Book on Tape, but it wasn't very stimulating. As it got hotter inside, I decided to strip off my clothes and start the new trend of naked ice fishing. Art quickly followed, and we both laughed at the cold metal of the chairs cooling our butts. Then I caught a fish! As I pulled it through the ice, we both gasped. Neither of us had ever seen a fish like this before. It was silver, about sixteen inches long, weighing around two pounds. I took out the hook and tossed the fish outside on the frozen snow.

About a half hour later, we were sitting naked, drinking beer, and there was a rap on the door. We both struggled to get our pants on. It was difficult because we couldn't fully stand up. Seconds later, a head popped into our little house.

It was a guy from the resort. He inquired, "Is everything all right? Is the heater working?"

We both answered, "Everything's fine, thanks."

Then to distract him from noticing we were half dressed, I said, "I caught a fish that I've never seen before. Do you know what it is?"

He said, "It's a Tulipe. It's edible, but most people smoke 'em."

We caught a couple of small crappies and left for our time-share. I tried cooking the Tulipe and found bones everywhere. Most other fish don't have bones in those places. I ended up throwing the entire fish away.

Another recreation that we enjoyed was watching porno videos. I always brought some to Breezy. More fun yet was when we brought our own video camera. We made a couple of our own X-rated movies with the camera on a tripod. It is still fun to watch them once in a while today. Another time, we went cross-country skiing in the woods. There were groomed trails. It was a warm winter day and the sun felt hot on our faces. Art had the camera and asked me if I would strip down naked. Then he would film me skiing cross-country. I was happy to comply, and he took a five-minute video of me skiing naked. I jerked off for the camera at the end of the shoot

We had a Jacuzzi in our room, and one time, we made passionate love in the Jacuzzi. Before we could finish, the maintenance man was pounding on our door, saying that our tub was overflowing into the parking garage below. By 2000, conflict between management companies erupted, and suddenly, we couldn't use any of the resort facilities, including the ice-fishing houses. The time-share groups had to build their own recreation center outside the gates of Breezy Point.

Chapter Seventeen

The Dogs

It didn't take long for me to see that Esther's generally a Democrat. That was good because I also tend toward being a liberal. For me, a conservative person is one who drives a minivan in the left lane at two miles per hour under the speed limit, effectively blocking any traffic going the speed limit or slightly faster. In my opinion, conservatives seem to be dominated by fear and seem to be unwilling to welcome change and progress. To me, they seem insecure. Unlike liberals, conservatives seem more likely to embrace the past rather than try to plan for the future. Of course, I'm sure a conservative person would think that I'm reckless.

* * *

I've had gardens most of my life, and I love to share my overabundance with those who're unable to garden. In early July, I'd harvest the best raspberries I've ever tasted and give them to Esther, Louise, and others. I'd often have too many tomatoes and green beans most years. Esther grew up on a farm, and one of her early memories was of her sister and herself doing the usual farm chores. I asked her if there were geese or pigs on the farm, but she said mostly they just had dairy cows. She liked animals and always wanted me to talk about my dogs.

From my five-year relationship with Derrick starting back in 1979, I've had White West Highland Terriers. When Derrick and I split up, each of us took one dog of the two male littermates we raised since 1979. I got Eddie. Eddie was very smart and not quite as stocky as his brother Winston. Eddie was very sensitive and never needed reprimands. Eddie would bark an alert every time Winston escaped from the yard. When I met Art, I felt that I wanted to have two dogs again. The fall of our meeting, Art and I drove to Fargo to pick up Nikki Sioux. My grand plan was to breed Eddie and Nikki. By the time Esther came into my life, Eddie was thirteen and really slowing down. I would show Esther pictures of the dogs at the lake. She laughed at Nikki sitting on the picnic table and Eddie swimming in the shallows. She grew up with farm dogs that stayed outside and lived in doghouses near the barns.

Eddie was fourteen in '94 and Nikki was six. Nikki was unusual because she only came into heat once a year. She was so discreet that the only way we knew she was in heat was from the reactions of other male dogs. She'd chase away almost any other male dog except for Eddie. Eddie would start to mount her when she was fertile, but he never really connected with her. Art told me one day that he thought Eddie was too Lutheran. By the summer of '94, hopes of Eddie becoming a father were becoming dim.

Art and I both had gym memberships. I was in Uptown fairly often, and one day, I had to go into the pet shop because there were Westie pups in the window. I told Art about them, and soon after, on our way home from the gym one evening, we stopped to see the puppies again. Art put money down on one, and we picked up the puppy a few days later. Art named him Kaiser Alexander Wellington.

Kaiser had a tough go of it for a while. Eddie was still king, but he was deaf and almost blind. Nikki wanted nothing to do with Kaiser and didn't want her succession to queen be muddled by this young puppy. Kaiser was Eddie's eyes and ears. Whenever we came home, Kaiser would go to where Eddie was asleep and quickly make nose contact with him. Then he'd jump back. Eddie was getting to be a crotchety old dog and woke with a mean snarl. Kaiser would then guide Eddie to the door and go out with him.

Nikki continued to be aloof. No one was training Kaiser the way Eddie trained Nikki. Kaiser was also insecure and had separation anxiety. It was interesting to see him follow old Eddie and mimic his parade around the perimeter of the yard and the scratching of the turf after urinating. The winter was hard on Eddie. By the spring of '95, Eddie was getting skinny, and patches of his hair were falling out. He was totally deaf and severely impaired visually. Up at the lake, there was a cornfield just behind us, and Eddie would wander into the field and get lost. I trained Nikki to go after him and bring him back, which she quickly learned how to do. That summer, eagles and hawks would circle above skinny Eddie. We dug a grave in late summer, knowing that he probably wouldn't make it into winter.

In the meantime, Kaiser warmed his way into Nikki's heart, and before his first birthday, he was going to be a father. I read up on birthing of dogs and tried to keep Nikki as happy as I was able to. We couldn't afford to have a lot of prenatal care, but I did my best to see that she had a good diet and regular exercise. The dogs had a strange habit of eating from my garden. All of them loved carrots and green peppers. Eddie particularly loved red tomatoes. He could find a red tomato even after I'd been through and picked all that I could find. It was a picture to see him with his white muzzle soaked in red juice.

Eddie continued to falter, and it became obvious that his enjoyment of life was minimal. Art and I had talked about the ending of his life. Usually, people euthanize their infirmed pets. I thought maybe if I just left him in the car with the engine running, he would fall asleep and die harmlessly. I even asked a patient, who was a fireman, how long it would take to kill a dog that way. He guessed about twenty minutes to a half hour. One early hot fall Sunday morning, I let the dogs out, and poor Eddie fell off the cement steps and could barely get back up. I took him in my arms and said good-bye. I carried him into the garage and put him in the covered back of the pickup truck in which Art drove then. I started the engine and closed the garage door. I went into the house and started crying. After about a half hour, Art woke up and asked what was going on and why I was crying.

I told him, "Eddie's in the garage with the truck running."

Art shed a few of his own tears. He said, "Turn the engine off because it could start a fire."

I walked out with the remote-control door opener and hit the button. What I saw next made me laugh. Here was Eddie sitting patiently, looking at me as if to ask, "Are we going to the lake soon or what?" He was more alert than I'd seen him in weeks. I picked him up and hugged him and cried.

The whole ordeal woke the neighbor next door, and she yelled from her porch window, "What on earth is going on?"

I admitted, "We tried to snuff Eddie but it didn't work." I learned later that carbon monoxide therapy is sometimes used as therapy.

My neighbor said, "Oh, you guys. Take him to the vet." I decided that she was right.

The next day, I made an appointment with the vet. Art and I both took that following Wednesday off. We decided we would take his body, and we'd drive to the lake and bury him in the grave we'd already dug. Our visit to the vet was strange. Eddie walked in as if he was going to the Promised Land. They missed his vein on one leg and had to go through a different leg. Then they put him out, and he collapsed in my arms. We wrapped him and put him in the truck and started driving to the lake.

He was in the bed of the truck; we were in the passenger cab. Two hours into our drive, I hear a loud, sad wail, which seemed to be coming from the back of the truck. Neither Art nor I were talking. We were consumed by our grief. I didn't say anything, and Art reached over and turned the radio up louder. He's never done that before. When we pulled into our land, I checked to make sure Eddie really was dead. He was by then. We buried him and walked to the picnic table to have a little lunch. An eagle soared right above Eddie's grave.

It was only then that I said to Art, "I heard him screaming on the way up."

Art replied, "I heard him too, and that's why I turned the volume up on the radio."

I chose to think Eddie was crying out from beyond to say goodbye. Art thought that he wasn't given enough anesthetic.

Chapter Eighteen

Puppies

The morning that Nikki had her babies, she was uncomfortable and restless. She paced back and forth. I couldn't tell if she needed to go out for a pee or dump. When I let her out, she started to dig a hole in the dirt near the house to make a cool spot to lie in. I got her back in the house and tried to clean the dirt off of her. I had my birthing book open and the telephone number of my vet if needed. It was Wednesday, my day off. Early in the afternoon, Nikki started panting and made some strange throaty noises. All of a sudden, both sets of our eyes got big. With one more guttural noise, Nikki passed a baby out. We both looked at the strange sight.

I was expecting a blind, bald, mouselike baby. Instead there was a transparent balloon about as big as a grapefruit but more oblong, with a white-haired baby inside. I knew that the surrounding membrane had to be pulled off. Usually the mother dog does this. Nikki wasn't at all sure what this was. I knew that it'd be up to me to get the membrane off. I broke it open with my fingernail and pulled it off the first puppy. My heart sank because the puppy wasn't breathing. I didn't know what to do. I started to instinctively stroke the baby's head, and all of a sudden, he took a gulp of air. He was alive.

As soon as Nikki saw that it was a baby, her mothering instincts kicked right in, and she started cleaning the baby. She had three more pups. Art came home after the first three and petted and reassured Nikki. I went to the kitchen to get some coffee.

Art shouted, "She's making weird sounds."

I yelled back from the kitchen, "She's having another baby."

Sure enough, there were now four. We waited for a few hours, but there weren't any more babies, and the placenta had been shed.

Nikki took to motherhood as if it was her ultimate goal. She was very protective and kept the pups well fed and cleaned. After a few weeks, we let Kaiser see his offspring. He enjoyed the babies, and when they could see and move around, he played with them. When the pups were weaned, Nikki weaned them into my schedule. She began feeding them only morning, noon, and night. I heated goat's milk and mixed it with pabulum. The puppies grew up in a small bedroom inside a plastic kiddie pool. In just a few weeks, they figured out how to roll out of the pool and run all over the room.

After a few more months, I took the two dogs to the vet for their annual checkups. I asked the vet when Nikki would begin menopause.

He laughed and said, "Humans are the only animals that go into menopause." The following spring, Kaiser nailed Nikki again, and she had three more puppies.

This time she was truly professional. Art and I were up on our sundeck one afternoon when Nikki came up to join us. I thought it was odd that she'd leave her newborn babies alone on the first floor. Nikki relaxed in the sun, but I noticed her ears were constantly searching for the faintest whimper of a puppy. I quietly slipped downstairs and peeked in on the babies. Each of the three puppies was tucked into a section of the blanket. Nikki had wrapped up each of them.

Esther always wanted updates on the puppies. I brought pictures to work and showed them to her. The dogs were pedigreed and healthy. They were easy to sell. It was harder to find good, compatible, and worthy owners. By another nine weeks, all the puppies were sold. I convinced Art that we should take the money and go on a trip. We talked it over and decided to go to Hawaii.

Chapter Nineteen

Hawaii

We planned a trip to Maui for the end of January. We had enough money for our flights and a guesthouse. We found a gay guesthouse and booked our accommodations. We were going for a week. We found a house sitter for Nikki and Kaiser.

From the beginning, the trip didn't go well. We were at the airport with plenty of time to spare. We checked in and were waiting to board. The bar across from our gate was open, so we went, and each had a double Bloody Mary. Our server was really hot. We felt bold enough to write our phone number on a napkin and gave it to him along with our money. Then we heard an announcement saying that our flight was delayed. As a matter of fact, we were asked to go back to the ticket counter and get lunch vouchers. The delay lasted several hours and put us six hours behind schedule. We got to Maui after dark and had to try to find the guesthouse. When we arrived, the caretaker was already in bed, but he got up and showed us our room. Then he gave us directions to the nearest liquor store, which would close in a half hour.

When we woke in the morning, the promised breakfast on the lanai was cancelled due to weather. It was cool and rainy. Our host kept telling us that it was unusual, and the next day was bound to be better. Every day was cool and threatening rain. We never once had breakfast outdoors. Art and I went to Little Beach, Makena, where we were able to tan and swim naked. We even saw whales not far from where we swam. The house that we stayed at was a big old traditional Hawaiian house. By midweek, all of the other guests left, and we were alone with Philip, the caretaker. We all smoked cigarettes back then. Philip invited us into the master suite for drinks, smokes, pot, and sex. It was like a scene from *Who's Afraid of Virginia Wolf?* We drank and talked and smoked cigarettes and pot.

Philip began to make a lot of insulting comments to Art, and Art finally got up and went back to our room. Then Philip started coming on to me sexually. He was going to make love to me now that we were alone at last. I wanted no part of sex without Art. I had to fight Philip off of me, and he was taller and stronger, and he was even drunker than I was.

By the time I got back to our room, Art was looking for a phone book and was ready to fly away on the next flight out. I told Art how I'd had to fight off Philip and that we didn't have sex. Art was so angry that he didn't know what to believe. Finally he calmed down. I suggested to Art that we lock our door and sleep off our intoxication. The next morning, Philip was there making breakfast as if nothing out of the ordinary had taken place. He even asked me if I would give him a massage later. I told him firmly that a massage was no longer an option.

We had one other encounter that shocked me. We decided to go to a nice Italian restaurant in Kihei. I was pretty stoned and a little drunk. We were seated in the dining room, even though the host wanted to seat us on the back patio overlooking the parking lot. We ordered drinks. As the server brought them to us, Art overheard him talking to the host, complaining that he had to wait on a couple of old faggots. After he brought the drinks, Art told me what he'd overheard.

I whispered to Art, "I think we should just get up and leave."

Art said, "I think we're obligated to pay for our drinks first."

I disagreed. Eventually, Art asked for the bill. He paid and we left. We drove to Burger King a few blocks away and bought food to take back to our room. It's incidents like this that lead us to make the effort to patronize gay resorts and establishments.

By the time we were leaving, the weather finally got better. It'd snowed on Haliakala every night, and there were flash-flood warnings. But now, it was hot and sunny. We got to Honolulu, and again, we had delays because our flight crew was late. We had to change aircrafts in San Francisco and arrived in Minneapolis / St. Paul in the early morning. It was thirty degrees below zero, and we had to sit on the plane another forty-five minutes because the gangway was frozen. The plane doors had to be thawed in order for them to open it. We still want to return to Hawaii some day. After all, how could it be any worse?

When I talked to Esther after that trip, I left out the attempted rape scene. I told her about all the rain and the drive up to Haliakala. I even mentioned the potato chip bag that we bought at sea level, which burst open near the top of the mountain because of the air pressure change. I talked about the drive through fragrant sandalwood forests and stretches of pastureland for horses.

Esther was still getting rides to my office from friends or taxis. Her mind was still sharp. One day, I was outside when I saw her walking toward my office. I pointed to the big brick duplex across the street.

I greeted her and said, "I put in an offer to buy that house from the estate of the woman who used to own it. She died over the winter." I envisioned moving my office to a much larger and brighter space.

When Esther heard my excitement over the brick house, she asked me, "When did you get that bee in your bonnet?"

I laughed because I don't think I'd ever heard that old expression before.

Chapter Twenty

Home Improvement—The Attic

Esther liked Bill Clinton. She knew he was smart. The economy was moving along well. Esther viewed his little stint with Monica Lewinski as the playfulness of his hormones. Since I'd decided to forgo insurance reimbursement and started doing my own massage, my life was easier. My business in the Clinton years was pretty good, and lots of people had disposable income, which could be spent in many sorts of self-indulgent ways. Massage was getting a respectable reputation.

Business was good but never great. I eventually had to say good-bye to Louise. Fortunately, we remain friends. I was still not advertising. Only patients who were already coming to the office knew that I offered massage as well as chiropractic.

* * *

Art's house was an "expansion." Upstairs was a large unfinished space. There wasn't any heat, and it had only rafters and studs. On the south side were two side-by-side windows. Because we enjoy naked suntanning, we decided to build a sundeck off the second floor. We planned it and had to get a permit. Then we built a cedar deck to code.

When the inspector showed up, he asked, "How are you going to access the deck?"

Art said to him, "We're planning to replace the windows with a glass patio sliding door."

He told us, "You should've gotten the permit to include the door."

He signed off on the permit anyway. For a few months, we crawled through the windows. Eventually, we cut through the stucco and put in a patio door. I designed a louvered railing system that allowed us privacy from everyone.

The following winter, I was in the attic, and I decided it wouldn't take that much work to frame up a couple of rooms and add a bathroom. Art was surprised by my ambition but agreed to a plan. We designed for the best use of the space, and I did most of the work. A friend completed the electrical work. Art financed the project. It took a few months, but the completed project gave a big boost to the home's worth. I had to rip out walls in the first-floor bathroom in order to extend pipes and waste stacks. I had previously replaced all of the galvanized pipes with copper.

After we were finished upstairs with the bathroom at Art's, I was able to finish the main-floor bathroom. I was able to reuse the wonderful old bathtub and keep the old tile floor. We replaced the large old window with a high little crank-out window. We had to stucco the outside opening, where the old window used to fit.

I always had more time than money when it came to home improvement. I learned as I went and often used resource books for plumbing, building, and repairs. I never had any fear about starting a job. If I had any reservations or concerns, I'd start the project with a cocktail! I did all my own finishing work. The truth is that while doing these jobs, one gets proficient at the end of the job. Sometimes you don't ever do that same job again.

Chapter Twenty-One

Gay Relations

When I first met Art, we were good friends. He was a good man and more stable than most of the gay men that I'd previously met. When I first began wondering if I might be gay, I looked around and sought out role models that I could look up to. In the sixties, I wasn't aware of any role models for myself. My sixth-grade teacher was the first male schoolteacher that I'd ever had. He was married, and even though I had some hope of finding something to model in him, he never openly cooperated. Fifty years later, he called me to reconnect, and lo and behold, he admitted to being bisexual!

As a young gay man in the fifties and sixties, I felt very much alone. It was easy to follow the majority and date women and play sports and grow up straight. But I was also a pretty boy. I was attractive but in an androgynous sense. I was also attracted to guys who were more androgynous. When the Beatles came to America, I fell in love with long hair on men. The hippie era reinforced the long hair. I loved to see young naked men, longhaired and beautiful, with nicely shaped bodies that weren't overdeveloped. My first love interest was a longhaired hippie man. His hair was reddish brown. He was slightly older than I but taught me a lot about giving and receiving sex from men.

I was once considered hot, and I had a lean well-muscled body as a result of many physically strenuous jobs that I'd had in order to put myself through school. When I was at the University of Minnesota, another student saw me on an intercampus bus, and as I found out much later, he considered me pretty. Just after Philip saw me on the bus, he went for counseling at Gay House. He walked in and saw me sitting on a couch. It was a coincidence that at the same time, I was staying there temporarily. We later became friends, and a few years after that, his story about seeing me, calling me pretty, realizing for the first time that he too was gay, and then coming out was published in the *Advocate*. It saddened me to hear ten years later that he died of AIDS.

I never thought of myself as pretty. I didn't spend much time looking at myself in the mirror the way some gay men did at the gym. I loved the story of Narcissus but didn't feel I had the same qualities to fall in love with myself. I think my father had difficulty relating to me because I was more of a pretty boy instead of a handsome son. I enjoyed boy and girl games equally.

Even in the gay world, I was given the title of "boy toy" for much of my coming- out years. I never related to that title. I wanted a meaningful and a wonderfully sensual relationship with another man, not to just be an object of desire. I was used to being hit on, and I was good at noticing guys who were hitting on me. My parents never gave me approval, but my face, body, and dick made me easily accepted in the gay community. Being gay was not always easy. I laugh at people who think that it's a deliberate choice. Who would choose to have themselves scorned, mocked, and humiliated by bigots?

It's no wonder that many gay boys and girls don't have a chance to develop strong self-esteem. The current American culture has a strong bias against gays. We're not good enough to marry, we shouldn't serve in the military unless we hide our true identities, and we don't have full rights of life, liberty, and the pursuit of happiness unless we conform to a straight world. We're not always entitled to health care through our partners. Sometimes, we can't even visit our own partners in the hospital when they're sick or bury their body when they die. We're sometimes treated like second-class citizens. Where do we get any strength for our self-respect? A straight friend of mine once asked me why gays had to have a gay pride celebration. At the time, I wasn't quick enough to respond with a clever answer.

But upon more thought, I think that a gay celebration is sometimes the only way to elevate gay self-esteem collectively.

* * *

After I was with Art for a while, I wasn't sure what our relationship should be. It was more than buddies but not as much as marriage. We were sometimes partners and sometimes on our own. We rarely shared our incomes. My first long-term relationship with Derrick ended badly. Then, I considered a relationship like a marriage, "'til death do we part." But one day, Derrick told me that I should find another place to live in order to make room for his new boyfriend. It took me almost five years to find out that Derrick had been cheating on me all the time. I was often home alone playing the drunken suburban housewife, hopelessly waiting for him to show up so that I could serve dinner. I knew that I never wanted that type of relationship again.

Art was different from Derrick in many good ways. Unfortunately, I was still noncommittal toward relationships in the beginning. There was a trust issue that always seemed to rear up. I liked to play around, and I felt playing around was okay as long as it was based on sex and not emotion. I was a couple of years younger than Art. I felt I had looks that appealed to a lot of gay men. I also needed other guys to want to be with me. It was important for me to know that a guy got a woody in the shower in the gym because he was fantasizing about me.

Art had reasons to be lacking in trust. When we were first dating, I went out with a drunken man that Art also knew. The drunk was pulled over and locked up for DUI. Another time, I was lying naked on the beach at BAB with a young stranger, and we were given tickets for improper clothing. I had to appear in traffic court to plead guilty before a sarcastic judge. Art somehow got a hold of the police records and read the full report. He located the other guy and talked to him regarding the beach relationship. One other time, I let a guy talk me into coming over to Art's house, where we played around. Art found out, and I finally agreed to never have anyone over his/our house. I've been true to that promise.

Oddly, almost every time I ever tried anything out of line, Art found out. Then he started suspecting me all the time, even when I didn't do anything bad. He began to think that my massage business was a front to have sex with young hot men. It wasn't. If I was at work later than usual, he thought I was playing around with someone. It was a wedge between us that I couldn't seem to get rid of.

Art and I had a relationship of understood monogamy. I liked to push the envelope, and eventually, I arbitrarily decided that if I didn't throw it in his face, I could occasionally play with other guys as long as I used discretion and protection, and I was safe. In our earlier days, we'd played with other guys together once in a while, and we usually had good times. As I got further into sex with Internet strangers, I gradually used less precaution and finally even abandoned protection. It wasn't until early 2003 that I crossed over my own line and had bareback (without any protection) sex.

Until that time, I had more concrete boundaries and didn't go out of my comfort zone chasing sexual fantasies. My work became a refuge for me from Art and from sex. My patients were also "my family." I wasn't interested in family sex and patients always remained off-limits. Esther was much like the mother that I no longer had, and she never judged me. I always appreciated that aspect of our relationship.

Chapter Twenty-Two

Aveda Rewards

At home with Art, I built on my cooking skills and my skills at home remodeling. My volunteer work was fulfilling but also depressing at the same time. I was amazed to see vibrant twenty- and thirty-year-old men and even some women deteriorate to death in just a year or two, sometimes less. I saw guys who had dementia so bad that they didn't know where they were or why. One man came for a treatment and told me that he had pneumonia for almost a year and that drugs were not getting rid of it. I gave him a chiropractic adjustment, and two weeks later, I saw him again. He told me that after that first treatment, the drugs finally kicked in.

The disease process seemed to affect all parts of the bodies. I usually only knew the people I worked on at the Project by first names. All through the nineties, most treatments were trial and error. I saw people a few times, and several weeks later, they were dead. Some became blind. Most aged very rapidly, got terribly skinny, and then died. Some were even carried to me by friends or wheeled in by wheelchair.

Some of the men and often the women seemed to progress more slowly. By the end of the nineties, better drugs were starting to be introduced. Regulars at the Project who came to see me became friends. I would try to lighten things up by trying to add humor. I got good insight into what it means to be HIV positive in our culture. There were many issues regarding employment and military service and healthy partners of infected persons. Even travel and immigration could be problematic. Benefits were sometimes available but frequently were not. The whole disease process was not fully understood, and little attention was paid to supplements and nutrition. I could suggest nutritional supplements, but most of the suggestions were beyond the financial resources of those who were sick. Often the disease came with deep guilt and fear. It was almost necessary to keep HIV a secret because the truth was an invitation to discrimination.

Even within the gay community, people took sides and snickered at the dumb guys who were bottoms, who succumbed to the virus. Safe sex was preached everywhere, and sales of condoms took off. Almost everywhere that gay men assembled, there were baskets of free latex condoms. Older guys like me were from the pre-condom days, when sex was spontaneous. For me, it seemed a lot like peeing with your underwear on. There was also a problem for anyone who was sensitive to latex. Early on, the definition of what was safe and what was risky was in flux. Usually the error was for caution. And of course, the young men and women just learning about sex felt they were immortal. HIV had a huge depressive effect on gay men in the eighties and nineties.

Imagine learning day after day that another friend was HIV positive. As I said before, I started reading the obituaries every day in order to try to keep abreast of the bad news. I went to funerals the way my parents did in their later years. In many ways, I was fortunate that I was often in a relationship during the early years of HIV. I often lamented about not being in the orgies at the bathhouses or not being invited to the all-out sex parties of the early years. When I first met Art, we practiced safe sex until we finally both got tested and found out we were negative. But I never got used to condoms and sometimes got a rash when I used the latex ones.

There was a medical doctor that specialized in treating HIV patients, who also started an educational AIDS awareness campaign. I was honored when he asked me to go on a few road trips with him, presenting chiropractic as a complementary therapy. Occasionally, a massage therapist and sometimes an acupuncturist came along with us. We spoke in St. Cloud and in the Twin Cities.

* * *

In 1996, I was sitting in my office when the phone rang. It was someone from the Aveda School. I was asked if I would be interested in teaching anatomy and physiology to Aveda massage students. I was referred to Aveda by a massage therapist who told them that I was a chiropractor who also did massage. Aveda was interested to have someone with my credentials. I explained that I never taught before and was told that it didn't matter. Then I was asked to prepare my resume.

I hadn't ever written a resume before. I'd been a chiropractor since 1979. All my previous jobs were short-term, working-to-get-through-school jobs. I put together a brief written history of my career. Then the HR rep told me that a few people at the corporate headquarters wanted to meet me. I agreed to meet and drove to Blaine. To me, a meeting meant that I was to meet with some people. I didn't dress for an interview; in fact, I wore blue jeans and a T-shirt as I often did in practice. I got there late because of rush-hour traffic. I was led into a conference room, and at the table, there were four people dressed in formal office attire. Of course they wore Aveda all-black clothing. They proceeded to interview me and ask me hypothetical questions. Only then did I realized it was a formal job interview

In the end, the obstacle seemed to be my pay, which I held firm on. I think it was forty-five dollars an hour.

The team voiced, "We feel that is more than we are willing to pay."

My reply was, "Well, it isn't worth leaving my practice for anything less than that."

I really didn't care one way or another if I got the job anyway. I was told that they would contact me the next day. I told them the truth, which was that I was going to fly to Sioux Falls the next day on a corporate jet to give a presentation with other health-care providers around the topic of HIV and complementary therapy. I wasn't sure what time I would be back.

I got a call the following evening. They said, "We've decided that you'd make an excellent instructor, and we'd like to hire you. Can you start teaching on Monday?"

I said, "No, I have to get the textbooks first. I could possibly start a week from Monday."

And so I began a two-year teaching career with Aveda. It was interesting at first. The classes were usually small. The students were not always the brightest. But once in a while, I had some students who were truly motivated. I was able to teach anything that I wanted, however I wanted to. I only got paid for the hours I actually taught. I got nothing for prep time and nothing for making up and correcting tests. It only took a few classes for me to realize that teaching, since I had gone to school, was now a performance art. Students expected to be entertained and had attention spans suitable for watching television. My understood goal was to teach students well enough so that they could pass the National Massage Board Exam. Of course, I never took that test nor ever saw any of the actual questions on the test.

As young students often do, they tried to get me off topic by asking me questions. Once during a pause in my presentation, hands went up, and I was asked, "Who is the most famous patient that you ever worked on?"

I thought about it and answered, "Probably the most famous person you might know is Colonel Klinck."

Confused eyes stared at me because no one knew who that was.

I finally realized that I was older than I thought. I said, "You know, from *Hogan's Heroes*."

Again, blank stares.

Finally, someone said, "Oh yeah, that old show on Nickelodeon."

While I was teaching, I wasn't able to take time before Christmas to go with Art to Breezy Point. I banked my week and decided to use it some other time when the school schedule wasn't so busy. By late spring, I searched and found information on St. Martin. It was a Caribbean island that was part French and part Dutch. It had beautiful beaches, good food, and friendly people. Some sources mentioned a nude gay beach. A few of my patients had been there or were thinking about going. I put in for a trade with the time-share folks and got a match at The View in St. Martin.

I was feeling rich with all my hours at Aveda. It didn't fully occur to me that I was a contract worker and that taxes weren't being taken out of my checks. Art and I planned and then commenced our first trip to St. Martin. Neither of us had any real sense of how long it was actually going to take to get there. It took almost an entire day to go and one again to come back. I'd only planned to be gone five days total from my teaching job. We got to St. Martin late at night and spent our first day driving around finding the beaches. After that day, we decided that we really liked it. When the saleswoman, Nanda, approached us to talk about buying into The View, we were already sold. There was a term for people like us; I think we were called lay-downs. We asked for a full week, every year. When she inquired which day we were leaving so that the papers could be ready, we told her we were leaving in two more days. She was shocked that we weren't staying at least a full week. But I had to get back to teaching.

We started going to St. Martin once a year and, with the free off-season reward week, more than once a year. We've had many memorable times there. In the meantime, Aveda also made me feel rich enough to get rid of my old Nissan and buy a new car. My poor Nissan had been through a lot. I was terribly self-conscious about my old car. A few years earlier, a Minneapolis Park Board truck backed over the hood of my car and crushed the front end. I got a settlement but used the money for other expenses because the damage was cosmetic and the car was old. It was such an embarrassment that I often parked several blocks away from things so that no one would see me get out of my beat-up car.

It was exciting to start looking for a new car. Unlike Art, I am a very impulsive buyer of nearly everything. I do some research, but once I go so far as test-drive a car, it's often the car that I'll buy. My new car was a Mercury Tracer wagon. I negotiated with a salesman and had specific requirements. I wanted a stick shift and a sunroof.

The salesman sold me a car but said there wasn't one exactly like that on his lot. He promised to get me one from another dealer. He asked what color I wanted. I could only tell him some colors that I definitely didn't want.

When I told Art that I bought a new car, the first thing he asked me was, "What color did you get?"

He laughed when I said, "I don't know what color I'm going to get."

It ended up being toreador red. It was a 1997 and is the car I still drive.

I liked teaching and I think I was good at it. The students seem to enjoy my methods. Better yet, they seemed to learn a lot. As time went on, Horst, the school's founder sold his company and school to Estee Lauder's company; and shortly after, the working environment seemed to sour for me. To save money, my hours were cut in half. I was only going to teach physiology. Another woman was going to teach anatomy. The students didn't like her, and they didn't learn very much basic anatomy from her. The staff at the day spa was getting loose, and there were investigations into staff dating students. I realized that I was only there because my background gave credibility to the training. I was soon told that I couldn't give any student a grade less than a B. I decided to cut my losses and gave notice to quit. I gave two-months notice but only in my last week was I asked what my reason was for leaving.

It was a chapter of my life that I treasured because it made me much more familiar with anatomy and physiology, which I had learned over twenty years earlier. I've heard from some of my Aveda students that they were able to pass the board tests without any trouble. I still run into some of my students even today.

Chapter Twenty-Three

After Aveda

My decision to leave Aveda scared me at first. I'd become accustomed to getting a fat paycheck, even when my chiropractic business was slow. But it turned out that when I was in the office more hours, I started seeing more patients. I also had more availability for doing massage. In April of '97, it really hit me how much tax I was going to have to pay from my Aveda earnings. It was way more than I expected, but I should've known better. At least now I had a new car and a time-share in lovely St. Martin.

We decided to take one free week, which we were awarded for a previous purchase of a week, in September 1998. It was Art's fiftieth birthday the day we arrived. I'd e-mailed ahead because I wanted to surprise Art by having flowers and a cake for his celebration. I asked Debbie at the front office for something in the fifty-dollar range. We arrived very late because we got trapped in Puerto Rico while changing planes. I winked at Debbie as we checked in. When we opened the door to our studio, a big cake box was sitting on the kitchen table. There were flowers around our studio, all picked from the manicured grounds.

Art opened the white box, and we both looked at the most beautiful cake with wide eyes and open mouths. We've never seen a cake like that before. All along the outside were ladyfinger cookies surrounding the body of the cake like a stockade. The cake was rectangular with a thick milky white frosting and various fruits, like kiwi and blackberries. We quickly found some plates and forks and helped ourselves to generous pieces. I started feeling anxious because

I was sure such a lavish cake would cost more than fifty dollars. I didn't want to appear to be cheap.

I went back to the office and asked Debbie, "How much was the cake? It's beautiful. Where did you have it made?"

Debbie answered, "We ordered it from Carlson's and Sons. It was forty dollars."

I gave Debbie fifty dollars and thanked her for the lovely cake. We rarely eat dessert at all, so we eventually brought most of the cake down to the office for everyone to share.

The next morning, we began what for us is almost a ritual when we're in St. Martin. We had our rental car, and we went to the grocery store as soon as it opened. We bought our supplies for the week and most of our liquor and wine. We put stuff away and then headed toward the gay-friendly beach, Cupecoy. We were carrying our towels, cameras, and food for lunch in a collapsible cooler. We decided to walk along the surf headed toward the far end of the beach on the narrow finger of sand that separated us from the sandstone cliffs, which towered on our other side. The last time we had been there, the waves were big but predictable. This day, the waves seemed menacing and very erratic. They sometimes crashed all the way into the sandstone cliffs.

We were happily walking the beach. All of a sudden, a huge wave crashed in. It hit Art, who was on the ocean side and literally knocked him right out of his shoes. He was lying in the surf, trying to get back up. His shoes were floating back and forth with the waves. All the stuff he was carrying was soaking wet with saltwater, including my new digital camera. I walked into the surf and helped him up. We were amazed and impressed by the power of the sea.

* * *

We often meet other folks in St. Martin. Sometimes they're gay, and many times, they're from other countries. We've met a retired navy man and his partner, a vice president of KLM, a retired English royal jeweler and his male Czechoslovakian spouse, many friendly

Canadians, many generous locals, and some very helpful straight couples. Many visitors of St. Martin are well traveled and affluent.

On our second winter break in St. Martin, we went to our favorite restaurant, Lynette's. We'd eaten there previously and enjoyed the local Creole flavors. It must've been in late January because the Super Bowl was on a television screen. There was a group eating on the raised area that sometimes doubles for the all-you-can-eat buffet. There was an older woman with coiffed gray hair, another tall older man, and a young (about twenty years old) lad. The group was completed by a couple of middle-aged men dressed in business suits. The young man kept cruising Art and me. I looked at him, and he was adorable. He eagerly focused on me, and I often looked away because I was nervous and blushing.

The older woman, whom I suspected was his mother, finally said something in Dutch, which I presumed was, "What do you keep staring at?"

The young man answered her in Dutch, "I am watching football."

Of course, he was lying. They were only about ten feet away from us. It was obvious to me that he was staring at Art and me. It also seemed strange that their table had three servers. The rest of the restaurant shared just one.

My curiosity was rewarded the next day when I read in the local paper that the queen of the Netherlands, Beatrix, was in town with one of her three sons and her husband. They were the ones at the table the evening before. When we got home from that trip, I looked up the royal family and read about them in Dutch on the Internet. One of the sons was rumored to be gay. He is the one I thought must have been staring at us. I had one of our best pictures blown up large and sent a letter to Prince Constantijn. I explained that I saw him staring at us. I mentioned in the letter that we vacationed at The View every year. I added that if he felt a need to get away while he was in St. Martin, he should call us and come relax with us.

I later discovered that Johann is the more colorful son. In any case, when the crown prince, Alexander, got married a few years later to an Argentinean woman, they honeymooned at a property serviced by the staff at The View. I still wave to all the yachts from our deck overlooking the ocean whenever I'm seeing boats that could potentially carry a Dutch prince.

Another part of going to the island became a tradition. I've always enjoyed smoking pot, and although I rarely have time to smoke it at home, it is a different thing while I am on vacation. Art is not as interested in it. One of the first times we went to Cupecoy, a native approached me.

He asked, "Is there anything that I can get for you?" Then he added quietly,

"Marijuana, coke, I can get you things."

I was a little wary of his intentions, but I didn't travel with my own marijuana. I asked, "Can you get me some marijuana?"

He said, "Yes, of course." Then he added, "I only sell it in fifty-dollar bags. How much do you want?"

Well, I am really a lightweight when it comes to smoking. A very small amount would've easily satisfied me. I didn't have fifty dollars with me that day on the beach.

I responded, "I'll probably pass. I don't have that much money with me today."

The good man replied, "I will get it for you, and you can pay me the next time I see you at the beach."

I bought a pipe the next day when we went to the market in Marigot. When we were at the beach the next time, I was smoking a little pot. I paid the man. The beach wasn't very crowded. After a few puffs, a man several feet away from us came over and struck up a conversation. He was on his honeymoon, and his new wife was a few yards from us, sitting on a beach blanket. This guy introduced himself and mentioned that he was related to a family who owned several car dealerships in Minnesota. I shared some pot with him and gave him some pot for later. After all, I would never be able to smoke all of it myself. Art and I were both puzzled when he returned to invite us to have dinner with him (and his new wife) later that evening.

He said, "We bought a big fresh fish at the market, and it's sitting in our bathtub. It's way too much for the two of us." Then he left to go back to his wife.

Art and I wondered if the wife would be as agreeable to dinner as the husband was. We also wondered if he wanted to have sex with one or both of us and where the wife fit in. We eventually declined the odd offer. The next day, the wife apparently found out about everything, and she scowled at us from a safe distance. The guy didn't even come over to say hello again.

When we were getting ready to leave for home, I still had over half of the marijuana left. I didn't want to throw it away, and I couldn't find anyone to give it to. Eventually, I came up with an idea. I used an empty plastic vitamin bottle, sealed the pot and the pipe in the bottle, and buried it in a spot where I could reclaim it again on the start of our next vacation. The first time I buried my treasure, I didn't have a good idea of where to leave it. Art suggested a French beach that had a lot of sand behind it. We buried it, and I drew a map of how to find it again. We came back just a few months later, and with the aid of my map, I was able to go to the spot and reach just under the sand and retrieve my pot.

This became part of our tradition on the island. Once we buried it on the grounds surrounding our time-share unit. We didn't find it again that next time. Another time, we buried it back at the French beach, and two days later, a hurricane blew all our landmarks away. There was also new construction in the area, so we never found it that time either. We decided on a new location that worked for several more trips. It was at a beach just below the sand by the third galvanized post holding up the chain-link fence from the beach entrance. Most recently, the adjoining property was sold to someone new, and they decided to replace the fence with a more permanent structure, which required a concrete footing all along the fence line. Again the pot was not there to retrieve. I have finally given up my habit of smoking pot. Maybe I am finally growing up!

* * *

I was more than happy to talk with Esther about our trips. I told her almost everything, just not the sexual things. I showed her many pictures of our trips. Art and I were always at our finest when we were traveling. I loved St. Martin because it gave me an opportunity to use my French, which I'd been fluent in at one time. It also seemed like a sexy and romantic island, and the ocean water was crystal clear and warm for swimming.

* * *

Art and I were not always going to St. Martin. Besides Hawaii and Breezy Point, we also took a trip to Sedona, Arizona. That was also a time-share trade from Breezy Point. That trip was using the fiftieth week, just like Breezy Point. It was mid-December. We flew to Phoenix and drove to Sedona after nightfall. We got there after 9:00 PM. Where we were staying, there was a festival of lights happening and displays of decorations for Christmas. All along the grounds of the time-share, various groups took space and decorated the inner courtyard. They charged admission and gave money to some charity. It was a balmy fifty degrees, but people there were dressed in parkas. There were lines and lines of people with lots of children. Luminarias lined the route to the displays.

The next morning, we opened the windows, and we were amazed by a landscape filled with one red bluff after the next. We expected John Wayne to ride up on his horse any minute. We spent several days touring and even went to some Indian ruins and ghost towns. We read all about the vortexes on the summits of the big red rock buttes. We had good food; one delicious dinner was at a Swiss restaurant. We went hiking through some of the foothills around the bigger buttes. Once home, I was disappointed that the photo shop toned down the reds of the rocks because they thought the intense colors must have been due to a camera flaw.

* * *

I started seeing Esther again more regularly. Esther wanted to know all about our trips. I had to laugh because one time, she asked, "Do you and Harold ever meet any nice available women on your trips?"

I thought she knew that we were a couple. She asked once or twice and then never again.

Chapter Twenty-Four

Bringing Dad Home

When my mother died in 1993, my sister Drena came for the funeral and stayed with Dad while she was here from Colorado. She confided in me then.

She said, "Dad and I talked about a lot of things. One thing I thought that you should know, Dad told me that you topped his list as the biggest disappointment of his life! He can't understand why you chose to be a homosexual. He thinks that Art influenced you into homosexuality." She went on, "I told him, David's your son, and you should love him regardless of who he loves."

I thanked Drena for telling me this, but it didn't strengthen my self-esteem. I suspected that Dad was uncomfortable with me. But when I heard this from her, I was very saddened. Much earlier, I had spent a lot of my time trying to gain acceptance from my family. I had even become a chiropractor like my father, hoping that this might help our relationship. I found a partner and settled down, owned a house, and had a career. I realized many years ago that "family values" was a hollow slogan for me. I would never measure up to what my father expected of me. I think my father was always uneasy with me even when I was a child because I was a pretty boy. I never chose to be gay, but I did make a choice not to live in a closet all my life.

With the outright acknowledgement of my father's disapproval, there was finally some freedom. I no longer had any need to try to impress my father. My own family wasn't going to give me approval so long as I was an obvious homosexual. So it was sad but also freeing to realize that it was always up to me to find my own family of support. Long ago, I made up my mind that I wasn't going to waste my time and talents trying to get my biological family to support and value my life. Now I was definitely on my own.

* * *

Dropping insurance reimbursement and adding massage therapy after my midlife crisis in '93 made me a much happier chiropractor. I didn't lose very many insurance patients and actually had more time to give better service. Dad was alarmed at first that I was doing massage. He looked at massage as being many steps down from a doctor of chiropractic. But I'd finally decided to make my own life happier without regard for what my family thought about it.

* * *

My father had his heart valve replaced in 1997. He came to my office earlier that year and complained about having congestion in his lungs and getting "stuffed up." He was having breathing difficulties. After asking him a few more questions, I decided to listen to his heart and lungs with a stethoscope.

I told Dad, "One of your valves isn't working in your heart. You need to see a cardiologist." And I added, "You will probably have to undergo open-heart surgery for valve replacement."

Of course, he refused. As a chiropractor of the old school, he looked at medical doctors as the enemy. Many of them felt the same way toward chiropractors. He did not trust them.

He protested, "I don't want to be put under anesthesia."

I tried to explain to him by saying, "This is now a routine procedure. Heart surgery is done on a daily basis, and it's something that surgeons are very good at." Then I added, "The results of not getting valve replacement will almost certainly lead to congestive heart failure and early death."

He finally relented and made the decision to at least get another opinion. My preliminary diagnosis was indeed correct. But while tests were being done for the heart valve, it was discovered that Dad also had prostate cancer.

Medically, it was deemed unwise to do much about the prostate until the heart valve was fixed. Because of my father's apprehension and fear, he decided to do nothing at all about anything. He continued to get winded very easily, and his stamina decreased dramatically. Art and I went on a short vacation to Breezy Point in December, and when we got back into town, there was a message on my office phone machine from my uncle Victor. He said on the message that Dad had been visiting another brother, Bob, who was in a veteran's nursing home when Dad collapsed. He was taken by ambulance to the hospital and was in intensive care for congestive heart failure.

I went to the hospital right away. There was Dad, looking pale and weak. Then he asked me how soon I thought they could do the heart operation. I told him that I was pretty sure he would have to be much stronger before they could try to do any surgery.

* * *

Since Mom died in 1993, Dad started a relationship with his high school friend, Jeanne, who he hadn't seen for fifty years. Jeanne had done well in life. She married a pilot, and she'd been a flight attendant for the old Pan Am. Her husband died shortly after Mom died. Jeanne always had a crush on Dad and named her firstborn Mark after my father. When she met my dad again after so many years, she was insistent on sharing her life with him.

The best thing about Jeanne, for me, was that she had an older sister. This sister had been married at one time but now lived with another woman. Jeanne, having been a flight attendant, was more affirming about other people's lifestyles. She was there with my dad to soften his hardness against me, and I soon learned that she was my best ally when it came to my gay lifestyle.

Jeanne was quite well off financially and had a home in a senior development in Sacramento, California. For several years, Jeanne and my dad shared an apartment in Bloomington, Minnesota, in the summer. They lived in Sacramento during the winters. After a few years, my father got rid of all his belongings and moved to Sacramento permanently. It was just before his heart surgery that he made the decision to give up the apartment in Bloomington.

* * *

While Dad was recovering from the congestive heart failure, Jeanne and my sister Paula were asked to have dinner with family. Dad was too weak to go. I decided to babysit my father while Jeanne went out for the evening. I thought it would be important for Dad to keep his spirits up because he was scheduled for open-heart surgery in about two weeks. I went to his apartment and made supper for him. I thought it would be fun to watch an old movie and picked out *The Long, Long Trailer* with Lucille Ball and Desi Arnez. I remembered seeing it at the drive-in movie theatre while on vacation when we were traveling with our own trailer. Dad couldn't remember ever seeing the movie, and he wasn't very interested in watching it with me.

After New Year 1997, Dad had his heart surgery. Most of the family who lived in town showed up at the hospital. The surgery was a success, and he came through it just fine. That spring, Dad started selling off and disposing his possessions. He gave me the family organ, a 1959 Hammond Spinet. I bought his old television, which was a huge color console with a record player inside. Later I found out that it didn't really work. It had to be attached to a VCR in order to tune in channels.

During that spring, my father started to treat his prostate cancer. He chose hormone therapy first without complete success. In 1998, he had radiation therapy, which seemed to quiet down the cancer for a while. Unfortunately, it also seemed to burn and scar his colon. In March of '99, he found out that his prostate cancer had spread to his bones, and he was now considered incurable. He was home for a wedding but had a difficult time. Jeanne called me from the hotel they were staying at after the wedding because he had complications from the treatment for his cancer. He had been injected in his abdomen, and he kept bleeding all night long from the puncture wound. I ended up taking him to the emergency room, where they were able to stop the bleeding. It took several hours before they could cauterize the wound effectively. Then he and Jeanne flew back to Sacramento.

It was in June 1999 that I got a telephone call from my aunt Ruth, Dad's sister, who also lived in California.

She talked to me about Dad and said, "Your father has become too much of a burden for Jeanne to care for him." Ruth thought that my father didn't have too much time left to live. She continued, "You children need to come and fly him back to Minneapolis while he can still get on a plane."

Dad was reticent about his condition. I had to call him and convince him to leave Sacramento.

Without any hesitation, I decided that it would be up to me to bring Dad home. None of my siblings wanted to go, and Dan's family was having a wedding that weekend. Also, no one else volunteered to give Dad a place to stay. My siblings were already in denial. I felt that I was the only one with presence of mind to take any action.

Art was on board with me too. He was willing to offer up our bedroom to Dad and Jeanne, whom I learned would be accompanying Dad. I called to arrange plane tickets. I was astounded to find out that last-minute tickets would be over one thousand dollars each way for each of us. I barely had that much credit on my credit cards. I checked for myself how to get there another way. I knew that we'd have to book a direct flight from Sacramento to Minneapolis, but I didn't need a direct flight to Sacramento. I got a ticket with Sun Country to San Francisco for $280 and rented a car one-way to Sacramento.

I left three days later after calling Dad and convincing him of the plans. I got on the plane without really knowing how to get to Sacramento and without knowing where the Sacramento airport was on the map. Jeanne explained to me that there was a shuttle from the airport to their house. Before I left, I went over my travel plans and told Jeanne that I planned to get to their house at around 7:00 PM.

It was a lonely trip, but I made it to San Francisco and got a rental car. It was rush-hour traffic. It took forever to get out of the city. I got on the freeway and drove for what seemed like hours. I had a few hours alone to feel the true sadness of taking Dad home to die. A host of other feelings came and went, many of them having to do with the shabby treatment I had always received from Dad in the past.

Just as the sun was setting, I got near Sacramento. It was annoying that the glare of the setting sun blinded me to most of the freeway signs. I missed the turnoff to the airport and was on the east side of the city before I stopped to get directions. All of that added about another hour to the trip.

I was very late getting to Jeanne's house. I wasn't really sure what to expect as I rang the bell. There was my dad, not looking like he was ready to die. Jeanne was there, and she was put off because I was late and hadn't called. I didn't have a cell phone, so there wasn't a convenient way to call her. Of course, Jeanne didn't think to turn down the dinner. She served up dry, almost blackened pork chops and I can't remember what else. Jeanne's sister was there too.

She took me aside and said, "I am indeed a lesbian. But of course, it would be better if nothing was said about it."

She was seventy-eight years old, and she was of the generation where the less said, the better in regard to sexual preference.

Dad was understandably melancholic. He was busy all weekend trying to tie up any loose ends and packing for his final departure. This was the same weekend that JFK Jr. crashed his plane and went missing off of Cape Cod. Dad was much more robust than I was expecting from Ruth's phone call. He was able to walk around and sit outside in the sun.

That next morning, Jeanne's sister was unable to turn the steering wheel of her Cadillac. I went out to see if I could figure out what to do. Somehow, I was able to get the steering wheel freed up so that they didn't have to call a repairman on Sunday. Dad complimented me on this accomplishment, which was unusual for him. Jeanne had a terrible cough and a lot of congestion. She was also running a slight fever. Jeanne seemed to me to be in worse shape than Dad was.

Monday morning was the big travel day. I had three tickets from Sacramento, nonstop, to Minneapolis. They were expensive. I tried to get a better price by mentioning the circumstance about my father. Northwest took note but wouldn't give me a break on the price because Dad wasn't in any official hospice program yet.

Jeanne, being a former flight attendant, was very efficient with packing and preparing for the flight. We arrived at the airport early. Our moods seemed quite somber. When we checked in, the young woman checking us at the gate looked for a long time at her screen. Then she said she'd read the notes on my file, and she upgraded Dad and Jeanne to first class! When she told me, I got so emotional that I started to cry. Of course, I was put in coach all alone.

The flight was nearly full, and I sat in an aisle seat next to a woman and another man. I talked to the woman during the flight and told her I was taking my ailing father back home to Minneapolis. I was just trying to pass the time while feeling very lonely. We were served food (it was part of the service back then in 1999), and to my surprise, my father walked back to coach to tell me how wonderful the food and service was in first class. It would be his only first-class airline experience. The woman next to me was amazed to see my father able to walk around the airplane after I told her that he was near death.

We arrived early in Minneapolis. I'd arranged to have Art pick us up. It was a hot day, and Jeanne had packed a lot of luggage, so we had to sit and wait for Art to show up with the car. Jeanne was not amused about waiting. We got to the house, and I was surprised that the bedroom we were giving up to Dad and Jeanne was still crowded with most of our stuff. Art and I quickly moved things upstairs so that they could settle in.

We had recently finished the upstairs, and even though it was very adequate spacewise, it wasn't air-conditioned yet. It would be Art's and my living space for the next several months. It was a big change to go from two gay men living alone with their dogs to having a dying parent and a friend sharing your house.

The first order of business was finding medical care. Both Jeanne and Dad needed to see a doctor. My dad had a doctor in Minneapolis, so it wasn't too hard to make an appointment. Jeanne needed to see a doctor, and I wasn't sure where to take her. I'd never been to one myself. I decided to go to Park Nicollet Clinic in St. Louis Park and took her to urgent care. After we walked in, they put her at the front of the line because she was having breathing difficulties. They took x-rays, told her that she had pneumonia, and immediately prescribed medicine.

I took Dad to his doctor and went in with him. The doctor had most of the recent test information. He told Dad that the prostate cancer had spread to his bones. The most that could be done would be palliative. Chemotherapy could be done, but it would only extend life a few more months at most and cause significant side effects. He told me about home-hospice care available through the county.

I made some calls, and within a week, I was able to get Dad into a home-hospice program. Fortunately, they would now pay for his expensive medications. The downside of hospice was that Dad couldn't have any treatment such as chemo or surgery to extend his life. He was able to have transfusions for low hemoglobin and get medicine for pain control.

Art and I began tending to Dad and Jeanne. Dad and Jeanne insisted that we accept money for "rent." While it was substantial, it didn't relieve the strain of constant caring from us. The hospice sent a nurse once a week and later offered such services as bathing, shaving, and babysitting when Jeanne wanted to get away. In many ways, it was a comfort to have Jeanne there so that Art and I could go to work every day. My routine became varied from back and forth to my home office to the grocery store to home. My chiropractic work and my night volunteering at the local AIDS project were my only refuge from the anxieties and exhaustion of tending to a dying parent.

We both enjoy cooking, and we were very creative in our meal planning. Often we would discuss over dinner what we might have the following day. Meal preparation was also our therapy. The goal was to devise nutritious, healthy, edible meals that tasted great, were varied, and interesting to a dying cancer patient. We had meals for three months and never repeated ourselves with the same meal twice.

We knocked ourselves out by making things like lamb shanks, spare ribs, chicken alfredo, beef stew, liver and onions, chili, minestrone soup, chicken and dumplings, grilled fish, and much more. We should've written a cookbook. Most of the entrees were accompanied by warm bread, a green salad, and sometimes a glass of wine.

The first weekend Dad was home, Paula, my youngest sister, said she wanted to take him to church on Sunday. He was able to walk on his own but used a wheelchair for going out of the house. Paula picked him up. It wasn't until after 3:00 PM that I got worried because he wasn't home yet. Phone calls to Paula went unanswered. I couldn't imagine where she would be and couldn't help but wonder if maybe she had to take him to a hospital. We finally heard back from Paula in the early evening. She said that she'd wheeled Dad all around Lake Nokomis and then made spaghetti dinner for him. She would be bringing him back soon.

Being a caregiver was an education for me. All of my siblings seemed to be in denial that Dad was terminal. To ease their minds, they did things with Dad that they wanted to do. Dad was a hostage to the needs of my siblings. Dad was unable to nap as he usually did. When Paula finally brought him home, he was really exhausted. That lasted into the next day. Maybe I was taking my nursemaid role too far, but I felt Dad needed more comfort care rather than more adventures.

My older brother Dan didn't like to visit because he didn't know what to talk about with Dad. Jim and Debbie came to visit but were told by Jeanne to come at times when Art and I wouldn't usually be home. Sister Carol drove in from Iowa with her husband, Dick, and the rest of the entire family. They brought food and beverages, but they arrived with such an entourage that the house felt like a three-ring circus. Art literally ran away as Carol took over our house. Carol brought a chicken dish and paper plates and plenty of food. Our small house hadn't seen such commotion since the holidays, when most of Art's family showed up for Christmas or Easter. When all was finished, Carol, Dick, and their kids left. I busied myself with cleaning up the mess. We lost a couple of forks that day, and I even went through the garbage, thinking they were thrown in the trash. They were never found. Again, I was so exhausted.

Days ran into weeks and weeks into months. I took Dad to get some of his business affairs done—usually on my Wednesdays off. Sometimes one just has to try to appreciate the humor in situations. Dad had some government bonds that he wanted to cash in. These were very old war bonds from post–World War II. Dad was getting so weak that now, to go out of the house, he always needed his wheelchair. So one very hot Wednesday, I loaded Dad into my little car and drove to a Wells Fargo Bank in the suburbs. We got to the bank and asked about cashing in the bonds. Of course, I knew nothing about bonds and how to cash them in, but I expected someone in a bank to know. The woman who helped us gathered up the bonds and took down the address that Dad was living at—Art's house. He had to fill out something about if taxes were to be taken out of the proceeds.

I asked the woman, "Does my father need to sign or notarize anything?"

She answered, "No, nothing else needs to be done. You should receive the proceeds in four to six weeks."

Dad kept getting weaker. The hospice nurse told us that he would have to get another blood transfusion. Again, I reserved my day off and made an appointment to take him to the hospital. The procedure takes several hours, so I made a morning appointment and planned to spend the day. I loaded Dad, the wheelchair, and Jeanne into my car; and we went to get a transfusion. It was pretty boring, but I was curious because several other cancer patients were there for the same procedure. I like to people-watch but was saddened by the plight of so many people.

The new blood really perked Dad up. He was doing so well that we decided we would "go out to dinner" and celebrate. Jeanne invited my dad's brother and wife, John and Joyce, to join us at a favorite restaurant, It's Greek to Me. As usual, we were running late. There wasn't any convenient place to drop off someone in a wheelchair near the restaurant, and I didn't want to pay a fortune for parking. I circled the block several times and then pulled into the bus stop and unloaded Dad and his wheelchair. As late as we were, John and Joyce showed up even later.

We had an enjoyable dinner. The staff was very attentive. Dad had been bound up with his bowels until we were just leaving the restaurant. I had to fetch the car, and all of a sudden, Dad had the urge. We had to race back to the house and get Dad to the toilet. We just barely made it.

* * *

When Art and I moved our stuff to the second floor, we thought it would be a comfortable space to spend the summer. We'd recently finished the upstairs expansion. We hadn't used the new space very much since it was finished. Art and I moved up there when Dad and Jeanne moved in that July. July in Minnesota can be very hot, sometimes even one hundred degrees. Art's house is across the street from a major freeway with no sound walls at that time. We thought we'd get good breezes from the windows and patio doors but soon discovered that the noise from the freeway was like sleeping next to the Indy 500 speedway. We were hot, sweaty, and miserable most nights.

We talked about this at breakfast one Sunday, and Jeanne suggested that we put in an air conditioner. She would pay for it. After all, there were two window units on the main floor, and it only made sense to have one upstairs. So after ordering a thru-the-wall unit and picking it up, we were ready to install it. That meant that we'd first have to cut through the stucco wall and frame in a spot for the conditioner.

In the meantime, our sleep was uneven, and sex between Art and I was virtually nonexistent. Sex never seemed interesting when we were so sweaty and sleep deprived. We usually fell into bed exhausted from every day's events. I had the old rocking chair in the sitting room, which I inherited when Mom died. I used to read the newspaper in that chair as a boy. It was a wide chair with sturdy arms that were also part of the sturdy wooden rockers. Since puberty, I had fantasies of playing with another man in that chair, visualizing all the sexual positions that the chair might accommodate. Now it was always too hot to even try anything in the rocker.

We decided to install the air conditioner on a Saturday. With the help of Jim, my electrician brother, and his two sons, we worked very hard. We ran into many little problems along the way. We finally finished later that evening and celebrated with a Saturday dinner. It was the first night that we were comfortable upstairs. After Jim, Debbie, and the boys left, Art and I went upstairs to retire earlier than usual. We ended up getting naked and playing around for the first time in weeks. We had marathon sex using the rocking chair as our prop. We never would've believed all the positions that the chair offered to have fun in. It was a truly memorable event, and I think both of us were satiated beyond our wildest fantasies.

The next morning, Dad, Jeanne, Art, and I were having Sunday breakfast. I happened to look up at the ceiling and noticed a wet spot.

I made the remark, "The air conditioner must not be draining properly. I'll have to slant the housing more so the condensation can drain to the outside of the house."

Jeanne piped up, "I thought something must be wrong. Last night, the chandelier was clanging and swaying for quite a while."

I looked at Art, he looked at me, and we both started laughing because we knew it was our rocking-chair antics, which had caused the chandelier to jiggle.

It's a grueling task to care for a terminal patient. It's even more so when that terminal patient is your parent. At the same time, one doesn't have time to really stop and think about it. Besides all the obvious chores, there were more mundane jobs that required work. I would never have been able to do it all without Art's help. He and my father often seemed to be on the same wavelength. Art would offer to get or do something even before my father asked for it. Art could tell when Dad's eyeglasses needed to be cleaned and if he wanted a "bump." We sometimes would have popcorn in the evenings, and Dad would have a beer. Other times, we would have a single alcoholic beverage, which Jeanne called a bump. Occasionally we had a glass of wine at dinner.

Jeanne was something else. Most people are fine and have good traits when you first meet them. After living with them, some of their true colors start to shine brighter. Jeanne was a prima donna. Her father had something to do with opera, and she thought of herself as an opera diva. She spent hours getting herself together in the mornings. She spent a lot of time painting her nails and went weekly to have her hair done. She had a standing appointment for her hair each week. Hospice provided an attendant to stay with Dad while she was gone. She looked good for her age. However, in the kitchen, she was almost worthless. I would have to rush home from work at noon so that Dad could have soup for lunch. Jeanne didn't want to risk breaking her nails on our electric can opener!

Gradually, that hair appointment took up more and more time. Finally, she admitted that a deceased girlfriend's husband, Sam, was courting her. He would pick her up at the door and drop her off hours later after the beauty shop and lunch. He was a nice guy, but it soon became obvious to not only Art and me but also to Dad that she was getting ready for Dad to leave. She had to have her next man in play for the future.

After about five weeks from the time Dad and I went to the bank, a letter arrived from the federal government. It stated that indeed, my father should have signed for the bonds and had everything notarized. He could still do it, but it had to be done in person. Dad was failing even more and was also sleeping a lot more. I thought that the sooner he signed, the better, because I was unsure if he would be able to do this later. I had to work Saturday morning, but I thought maybe we should try to get this signed and out of the way that same day. I went to work and called around to several banks. Most of them were either closed or didn't have a notary on staff Saturdays. I finally found a bank right on Nicollet and Lake Street that had a notary, but they were going to close at 2:00 PM.

I rushed home and got home around noon, only to find my uncle Victor was visiting. Dad was still in his pajamas and hadn't eaten lunch yet. I tried to impress upon everyone the urgency of getting to the bank before it closed. Victor decided he would come with Dad and me to the bank. I tried to hurry everything along, but in my mind, things were moving at a snail's pace. Traffic was even very slow. Why is it that when you are in a hurry, obstacles pile up to slow you down. We arrived at the bank at 1:50 PM and got Dad into a wheelchair and into the bank.

We entered the bank. I was totally freaked out. It was the first of the month. This was an inner-city bank. There were literally well over a hundred people in lines waiting to cash welfare checks. Most of the people waiting were anxious, ethnically diverse, and very few spoke English. I think my uncle also flipped out. He is a suburban born-again Christian man, who is not used to being surrounded by crude immigrants speaking foreign languages. Somehow after many minutes of waiting, he was able to get the attention of an employee who'd expedite a notarized signature. I had to shake my head and laugh at all the obstacles that had to be overcome in order to die.

* * *

There were other irritations to deal with. My father's sister Ruth started calling long distance from California to see how Dad was doing.

After several calls, she finally said, "I want to see your father near the time of his death because I can't afford to visit twice. I was hoping to see Mark out and go to his funeral at the same time."

I said, "I think Dad would prefer to see you before he died, while he can still share some quality time with you. I think you should come sooner rather than later."

Ruth ended up visiting about two weeks later, around the same time that my sister Drena also came to visit from Denver.

I enjoy Ruth, and we had several meals together with her. Neither Ruth nor Drena stayed with us. Ruth stayed with John and Joyce, and Drena stayed with Paula. Ruth admired Art's house and gardens. She took notes when I made a huge pot of chili. Ruth also took some cuttings of a red-twig dogwood that we had in the yard. I always liked Ruth, and I think she had a very nice final visit with Dad.

Drena came by almost every day too. Once, Dad had to have another transfusion, and I had to work. I allowed Drena to take him to the hospital. It seemed getting there wasn't a problem. Coming back home, Drena was unable to get the wheelchair with Dad in it up the front cement steps. As a result, the wheelchair tipped and Dad fell off of it and onto the pavement. Fortunately Dad wasn't hurt, just a little shaken up.

Evenings were usually spent around the television. Even deciding what to watch on television was problematic at times. We either watched broadcast TV or rented videotaped movies. I tried to get movies that were interesting, which we hadn't previously seen. One time, I remember picking out two movies at the video store. I thought that I'd made a good selection. When I got home and popped the first one in, it was a foreign film in another language, subtitled. That seemed like too much of a chore for entertainment. So I put in the second one, and it started out fine. Very soon however, I realized that the movie was about a detective searching for a woman who was caught up in a snuff-movie production. Not really the most uplifting kind of movie you'd want to watch with a dying parent. I left the movie on, but it became obvious that everyone watching the movie were watching under duress. We finally all decided to go to bed early rather than finish the movie.

Televised programming was even more unpredictable. Once we watched a television show about a hospital detective who had to deal with a terminal cancer patient who decided to commit suicide. I can only wonder what Dad felt while watching this episode. On weekends, Dad took the remote control and was in charge of programming. Sometimes it was an easy decision for him, like watching tennis for hours. Dad used to play tennis in high school and beyond. However, other times he would continuously change channels, never focusing on what the channel had to offer before switching it again.

Relatives would call, even those whom I hadn't talked to in years. They would ask me how Dad was doing. Whenever possible, I would just say that I thought Dad was doing pretty well but then offered to let them talk directly to him. Often this would startle them, and they'd become speechless.

Art and I often asked the hospice nurses how long this could go on. It was awkward to try to care for Dad and, still, to try to get a feel for how much longer you needed to keep things together. The nurses never gave us any clear time frame. Art and I had planned a trip to Palm Springs long before Dad came to live with us. This was to occur in November, the first week. Toward the end of September, we were getting anxious. We didn't want to leave Dad and Jeanne alone in our house while we went on vacation. What if he were to die while we were gone? We didn't have long to worry.

It was a warm Sunday, near the end of September, when Dad, Jeanne, Art, and I were sitting down to brunch. I got up to get some more coffee. I poured the brewed regular coffee, and then I asked if Dad and Jeanne wanted more coffee. Dad and Jeanne always wanted decaf coffee. Since they didn't drink that much coffee and Art and I drank brewed coffee with caffeine, I bought them instant coffee in a jar when I went grocery shopping. Now I shopped at least twice a week and always asked if I could get them anything. Usually they never made any demands.

So I was totally surprised when Jeanne lashed out at me and said, "I hate instant decaf coffee. I never want it anymore—ever. You can give the rest of the instant decaf coffee to Art's mother."

I was stunned by her rudeness. I left the table and went out to the backyard and cried. Shortly after that, Art came out and joined me.

He asked me, "What's wrong?"

I said to him, "I just can't deal with Jeanne anymore. She's so ungrateful. When I serve something special for them, she doesn't compliment me."

Rather than a compliment, she would make a hurtful statement like, "If you want good lamb shanks, you should go to It's Greek to Me" and "If you want good ribs, try the Market Barbeque."

I was at a breaking point.

Art totally sensed this, and after talking to me in the backyard, he said, "David, I understand you. We're going to have an intervention—right now!"

Dad had retired to the bedroom, and Jeanne was in the living room. Art entered the living room and I followed. Art was red-hot mad, and I was pale-white scared. Art started talking to Jeanne, and it wasn't long before they were both shouting back and forth.

Art yelled, "Jeanne, you're a selfish bitch. You never offer to help in the kitchen. And you don't even thank us for the meals we make for you. You're a freeloader."

Jeanne screamed, "I don't feel welcome in your kitchen, so why should I even try to help clear dishes or cook?"

This went on for several minutes, and I couldn't help but wonder what Dad was hearing.

Jeanne immediately called Paula and asked her if she'd put her and Dad up for a while. Paula agreed instantly, and by the time I came back home for lunch on Monday, Jeanne and Dad had moved to Paula's house, leaving neither a note nor a word of good-bye. Jeanne neglected to take Dad's oxygen supply tank. It was kind of weird to walk into the house that had been a source of so much strain not too long ago, and then suddenly, all was quiet. I felt as if a huge burden had been lifted from me. Later, I thanked Art for being so direct with Jeanne.

What happened after Dad and Jeanne moved to Paula and Jeff's house was a real eye-opener. My siblings, who'd been barely supportive of Art and me taking care of Dad, immediately started showering Paula with deliveries of gifts and flowers. My father's minister, who'd come to Art's house under the strain of being in a gay house, freely came to Paula's house and often brought communion. I cooked on Wednesdays and brought over meals for the four of them—Paula, Jeff, Jeanne, and Dad. I came to visit after work many times a week. Art, under the orders of Jeanne, wasn't allowed to visit. Of course, Art never wanted to run into Jeanne again. We discovered that Jeanne, in order to explain the sudden move to Paula's, told the family that Art and I were alcoholics, and so it was necessary for them to move.

* * *

Soon after Dad got situated at Paula's, he asked me to bring Art to see him. He asked us both to come on a Saturday, when Jeanne would be away. He wanted to talk to us in private. There, in the back sunroom, he spoke to both of us with a clarity that only comes to a terminally ill person near their end.

He said to us, "I've never been treated so well as when I was at your house. Your meals were out of this world and fit for a king." Then, addressing Art, he said, "I've grown fond of you, and I hope we can remain friends in spite of what's happened with Jeanne. I know she can be a difficult pill to swallow."

Then he looked at me and said, "Dave, I am proud of you, and I respect you and your relationship with Art. It seems like you're always able to get things done, and I really admire that in you."

It took a big man to say what he said to us, and I was very close to tears because of his admission. It probably saved me years of therapy for him to finally accept me. It was important for Art to hear it too. It's unfortunate that it took the specter of death for Dad to get to this point.

* * *

Dad continued to live at Paula's house until early December. During those last three months, he began to eat less and sleep more. He had to get recertified for hospice care in October. On December 7, 1999, I went to visit him after work in the evening. It was a Tuesday. Paula greeted me at the door.

She said, "I think Dad's in a coma."

I entered the bedroom and saw him lying very still, eyes closed. I was just about to leave when his eyes opened. They were very glazed, and I didn't think he was really able to see anything. I knew the time was coming soon for him to pass.

I said softly, "Dad, you have put up a good fight but there is no longer any reason for you to struggle. We are all going to be okay.

You have done all that you can, and if you want to leave us now, we'll be all right. We're ready and it's okay."

I knew as I left that he wouldn't be alive tomorrow.

I said to Art that night, "I think I should call Drena."

But he said, "Why don't you wait 'til tomorrow so that you'll know for sure."

I got the call early the next morning from Paula, who wanted me to come over; she thought that Dad was dead. It was a warm, foggy December morning, and I drove the short mile to her house. I'd been assigned the responsibility by hospice to pronounce Dad dead.

It's a strange thing to see your parent dead. There's still some body heat, but it's as if no one's home. A body doesn't die and decay all at once. Parts of it continue to live. Although I could see there wasn't a pulse or a breath, I had to work to close his eyes and push his jaw together. I'd never seen a body so soon after death, and I had an eerie notion that he would suddenly lift his head as he had done many times before and say, "Dave, is that you?" Of course, it was my day off, Wednesday.

Chapter Twenty-Five

After Dad

For some odd reason, there was a lot of anxiety surrounding the coming of 2000. People thought that after the stroke of midnight, nothing would work anymore. A lot of the insecurity revolved around computers. Most computers apparently weren't programmed to read beyond 1999, and people worried that records wouldn't automatically adjust to a new century. Funny, when 2000 rolled around, everything kept going like it always had.

* * *

When Dad died, there were a lot of loose ends to be tied up. All my siblings who lived near Minneapolis arrived. Dad was to be embalmed by my nephew-in-law, who worked for a funeral home in Waverly, Minnesota. Arrangements had to be made at the church and the mortuary. The obituary had to be drafted and sent to the paper.

Writing the obituary was a mind-boggling task. There were eight of us trying to speak at once while the mortician tried to write up a proper obit. It rambled on and didn't make use of good grammar. For myself, if I didn't see it written down, I couldn't comment. My family included my partner Art, as a survivor, in the obit. Then we had to pick out a coffin, a small printed prayer and personal information, and a charity for memorials. While this was going on, brother Dan took me aside.

He said to me, "I know I was designated as the executor of Dad's will. I think that you should do it because you know more about Dad's finances."

I knew that was a cop-out because Dan owed more to the estate than he'd get back; however, I couldn't say no. So I agreed to take on the task. The days leading up to the funeral, I had to get Drena back here from Denver, and we had to settle on a day where most of us could be there for the burial. We settled on Saturday.

The funeral was okay even though I was disappointed. My father was eighty, and he'd led a good life. I wanted a celebration of his life with some joy. The Missouri Synod Lutheran minister made sure that wouldn't happen. He rambled through his service, saying that Dad was dead when he was baptized as a child, and only now does he live again. Dad's younger brother, John, gave a talk, which was the best of the morning. He mentioned Mom and the heroic war efforts of Dad and said publicly that Dad paid the tuition for him to go to Northwestern Chiropractic College. It seemed odd to me because I had to pay my entire tuition myself. Then Paula stood up and gave an extemporaneous presentation of the last days of my father.

Paula was speaking in her own and our traditional family church. This was the same family church, which boasted adult religious classes teaching members how to shun evil, which included homosexuals. Paula failed to disclose the fact that Dad spent half of his dying days in Art's house. In fact, she went through her entire speech without giving Art any credit at all. The reality was that both Art and I went above and beyond duty to care for Dad. The rest of the service was much more a Jeanne production and not a celebration of Dad's life.

And if that wasn't enough, the Ladies Aid of the church was serving a light lunch in the church basement before the procession to the cemetery. All the church ladies had by now read the obituary, and they focused on the fact that David wasn't married and had a male partner. Some of Art's sisters showed up, and we all sat at a table together along with a few close friends of mine. It seemed as though the church ladies were practicing what they had learned at services—how to shun homosexuals. I was so preoccupied with greeting old neighbors and family friends that I was unaware of the ostracism going on at our table. I felt really bad when Art told me about all the mean and prejudicial things that he had to endure. To this day, he won't have anything to do with my family. And because of that, I rarely do anything with my family either.

At the cemetery, we stood around the coffin while a bitterly cold winter wind whipped around our shoulders. I was numb from the frigid wind and numb from the cold reception that I felt was offered to Art and me. I was also relieved that this chapter of my life was now ending. The stress of caring and wondering when my father would die was finally over.

There were other things to finish before all was done. One problem that came up was that of headstones. When Mom died, Dad put an inscription on her headstone that only gave her name, birth date and date of death, with an added line saying "wife." Dad said that he wanted his stone to also say husband, father, grandfather, and great-grandfather. My "gay" mind said that since these stones were for posterity, it was only fair that Mom's stone should also include mother and grandmother. So I had a go-around with the cemetery, insisting that Mom's stone be amended at the same time they were engraving Dad's stone. Of course, it cost extra money, and most of my siblings thought it was an unnecessary waste. But it was necessary for me. I finally got what I wanted in April when the ground thawed.

Chapter Twenty-Six

Diabetes

A few weeks after the funeral, Art and I started to put our house back together. We had lots of high-fructose soda pop around in case visitors wanted refreshment. Since I hate to throw away food, I decided that I'd drink some of that soda myself and gradually get rid of it. Through the end of December and into January 2000, I drank one, two, and even sometimes three cans of soda each day. Until this time, the only soda I drank was diet and only as a mix for vodka or rum. In early January, I started getting very weak and lethargic. I was always thirsty, and at night, I was getting up almost every hour to pee.

With my training as a chiropractor, I knew that these symptoms were indicative of diabetes. Of course, my first instinct was denial. Then I thought that maybe it was just a temporary condition, like gestational diabetes. I bought all the "miracle water" (water with a high level of minerals) that was on the grocery store shelves and stocked it at the side of my bed. I got up every hour to drink water and go to the bathroom. My mind got foggy and seemed to have a weird buzz about it. I lost some weight.

Art and I were scheduled to go on our annual vacation to St. Martin the end of January, and I decided that a trip was really what I needed to deal with my stress and diabetes.

I was working on Dad's estate and had most of it figured out. Brother Dan owed the estate over four times what he would be getting in his one-sixth share of inheritance. He also owed interest. I decided the best way to approach the situation was to give each sibling an itemized statement of what the estate consisted of and what Dan owed. Until Dan paid up (which he said he could do after he sold his house, and he was planning on doing that anyway), he was to pay his monthly interest starting with the eldest, Drena, and each subsequent month going down the line until he paid the interest amounts owed to the estate.

Art and I booked a flight that year with Sun Country, which flew from Minneapolis to St. Martin almost nonstop. There was a stop in New York City going and Puerto Rico and New York City coming back. The flight was about seven hours long. I was weak, thirsty, and had to go to the lavatory every thirty minutes. I finally told a flight attendant to keep bringing me water throughout the flight. We had a relaxing time in St. Martin, and the sun helped me a lot, but my diabetes only seemed to be getting worse. On the flight home, we were sitting in an aisle and middle seat. The passenger at the window went crazy with a panic attack and started pulling and pushing the passenger in the seat in front of him. Then he started verbally assaulting that passenger for reclining their seat too far. Finally, a flight attendant escorted the man to a different seat, further to the front of the plane. I was in agony enough because of my high blood sugar. It was a relief to have an open seat next to me.

Once home, Art bought me a blood-sugar monitoring kit and I took a reading. It was over 500. A reading over 120 isn't good. I decided I'd have to go see a medical doctor. Easier said than done. I called around to several doctors whom I knew to have good reputations. The answer was always the same. Dr. so-and-so wasn't seeing new patients or didn't see anyone without insurance. Of course, I didn't have insurance. Finally, I called the clinic where Art goes. I told the receptionist that I was diabetic and that I needed to see a doctor to get my blood sugar regulated. She made an appointment for me the next day.

I'd never been to a doctor except for one time in Boston. I was assigned to a rookie woman doctor. First, a nurse trainee saw me.

She asked, "When were you diagnosed with diabetes?"

I answered, "I diagnosed myself."

Then she said, "You don't really know if you're truly diabetic because a doctor hasn't diagnosed you."

I said to her, "But I am a doctor."

Then my doctor entered the room and introduced herself. I repeated my diagnosis to her and she said, "I will determine whether or not you have diabetes."

She did a blood test much like I do, and the reading was now in the high 400s. She came back and announced, "You definitely are diabetic."

Then she started to ask me health questions. She asked, "When was your last physical?"

I replied, "At forty-nine years old, I've never had a physical."

She was incredulous. She next asked, "When were your last immunizations?"

I answered, "I've never been immunized." After a moment's thought, I added, "Wait, I did have a tetanus shot in 1964."

She was at a loss as to how to proceed. I really wanted to say, "Just give me the medicine and let me go."

As if to read my mind, she said, "I can't just give you medications because you could have kidney disease. I think you should be admitted to a hospital."

I replied, "I can't go to a hospital because I have patients to see tomorrow, and I don't have insurance anyway. I can't take time off to be in a hospital."

She set up an educational appointment with a nurse the following week. In the meantime, nothing was done for my high sugar numbers.

* * *

Diabetes has been around a long time, and its management has been a mainstay of medicine for at least a century. My expectation was that the medical establishment probably knew everything about the disease and could easily manage the condition. I was so wrong. My appointment with the nurse was about seeing if I could use my meter correctly and then teaching me how to document my readings. Finally, we discussed medications.

I said, "I want a medication that will work with my body to produce more insulin, not just a chemical synthetic to trick my body."

She thought a while and replied, "I think Prandin, a pancreas stimulant might be what you are looking for."

So I started taking Prandin. It was a new drug, and it didn't come in a generic formula. It's also unusual because it should be taken thirty minutes before a meal. So I had to start timing my medication to when I would be eating. After a few weeks, Prandin seemed to be getting my blood sugars in better ranges.

Being diagnosed with diabetes at the age of forty-nine was devastating to me. Since chiropractic college, I'd given up white sugar and white flour almost totally. I had a balanced, good diet, and I did most of my own home cooking or ate Art's home cooking. I was fairly active, but I'd given up my gym membership. Since caring for my father, I didn't have time to go to a gym, and my level of stress was extremely high. I wasn't fifty yet, and suddenly my body, which had been on automatic function, was no longer working for me. I felt betrayed. I felt vulnerable. I was angry that my perfect body had stopped performing perfectly. I was embarrassed because the healthy attitudes that I tried to project to my patients were not healthy enough to save myself from disease. I didn't have health insurance.

I tried to rationalize that my mom had adult-onset diabetes and that some of my father's siblings were also diabetic. So I could use the heredity excuse. The medical community kept up the mantra that diabetes was chronic and progressive. According to them, it's a downward spiral leading ultimately to insulin, limb loss, blindness, kidney failure, and death. It scared me enough that I looked into medical insurance. I applied at two different companies. I was turned down after my blood tests came out less than perfect. Finally, I got into a program with the State of Minnesota. It was expensive and didn't cover preexisting conditions for six months, but it was the only thing I could get.

Then I found out that my insurance didn't want to cover Prandin. They insisted that I try the cheaper generic Metformin. I refused, and when the doctor wrote a note saying that I was unable to take Metformin because of kidney damage, they agreed to pay part of the Prandin. I'd never previously taken a prescription drug in my life, and I was unfamiliar with how to order them from the pharmacy. Art helped me navigate the process. I started to feel as if I was suddenly dependent on the pharmaceutical companies.

* * *

When 2000 began, George W. Bush was sworn in as president. I was shocked that a dumb, rich frat boy won the election. Actually, I never believed he'd won. It was so close in Florida that the Supreme Court ended up giving Bush the win. Gore won more votes. There were so many shenanigans surrounding Florida that I think most people were deceived into thinking Bush truly won. While it was a fact that the economy had begun to deteriorate in the last year of Clinton, the pace accelerated markedly when Bush took over.

* * *

In March, I needed a vacation again. I'd banked my time-share week at Breezy Point. I talked to Art, and we put in for an exchange for a week in March. Ten days before we were planning to go, we received a confirmation for a resort in Cabo San Lucas. We traveled to Mexico. It wasn't at all what we were expecting. Our resort was huge. It had several swimming pools. It was located right on the Pacific Ocean, but there were thunderous waves and deadly rip currents. Ocean swimming was strictly forbidden. Food was very average. A walk to town was through a corridor of begging poor and phony policemen. The town of Cabo was full of young American students on break spending daddy's credit cards and pretending to be adults. They drank too much and smoked cigars. Restaurants were very expensive and served the usual Mexican fare.

After a couple of days at the resort, Art and I were invited to a sales presentation with the lure of a bottle of tequila and a gift certificate to a restaurant. Our salesman was Carlos. He sat with us for a frugal lunch.

As I got out my Prandin, he asked, "What are your pills for?"

I revealed to him, "I have diabetes, and I take these pills to help keep my blood sugar low.

He followed up by saying, "There's a plant that grows in Baja that's used by native Mexicans to treat diabetes and cancer. It's called melon de coyote. I'll bring some to you during the coming week."

The promised tequila ended up being a six-ounce miniature bottle.

Halfway through the week, I got a call from Carlos, saying he was at the front gate and that I should come and get the herbs. The front gate was about four blocks from where our unit was. I walked over and out the front gate. Carlos was waiting in an old, World War II, German-jeep convertible with the top down. He gave me a jar of coyote melon and a large baggy of dried damiana leaves. I thanked him and proceeded to walk back through the entrance toward our room. There were armed guards in the lobby, and when they saw me, they seemed to scurry toward a telephone. I kept walking. Soon it occurred to me that the damiana looked just like a bag of Marijuana.

When I got to our door and entered, I blurted out to Art, "The police might be paying us a visit shortly." Fortunately, they didn't arrive.

I didn't want to end up in a Mexican hospital, so I packed the herbs in our suitcase and didn't take any of it until I got back home. Neither Art nor I cared for Mexico. When we checked out, the staff was so distrusting that they sent a maid to count everything in the unit we occupied to make sure we didn't steal anything. They had our credit card numbers for God's sake, and who wants some cheap tin forks anyway? Mexico didn't leave a good impression on us.

Once home, I began to research diabetes with the hope of beating it. I took my Prandin and exercised. I also took the coyote melon. It was very bitter and woody, and it was difficult to break off an edible piece. Whatever I was doing seemed to work to get my diabetes under control. I was still angry that my body was "inferior" and subject to disease at all. I read everything I could find on the Internet about diabetes and joined the American Diabetes Association. I went to a class on nutrition and realized that my training was superior to that of the medical dietician's. When I mentioned coyote melon to my doctor, she had a fit. She warned me that I could be doing serious damage to my body by straying from regular protocols. I told her that's why I hired her—to insure that my deviation didn't adversely affect my body. She asked me not to mention my herbal experiments to her ever again.

I was forty-nine, and my reward now was to finish life as a diabetic. I hated the notion. I was still reading obituaries and never liked reading "died of complications of diabetes." I found myself constantly sticking my fingers to draw a drop of blood in order to check my blood sugar levels. I had to remember to take my Prandin before every meal. Art bought a treadmill for me, and I began walking three or four miles every day. And, I experimented with my coyote melon. I also figured that some spices and foods would have a beneficial effect on blood sugar and that others may be detrimental. My whole existence became a laboratory. I tried various supplements and exotic cultural food recipes. The spices of India and Thailand seemed to be generally helpful. Red pepper, garlic, curry, and cinnamon seem helpful. Fenugreek, bitter melon, cumin, and ginger also seem to have a positive effect. Even calcium and vitamin D tend to lower my blood sugar. If we went out to a restaurant, I sometimes forgot to bring my Prandin. The first time this happened, I decided to order a gin martini as a substitute. I'd read somewhere that Juniper berries were a tonic for the pancreas. It seemed to work for me as well as Prandin. Of course, I could only tolerate one martini.

The American Diabetes Association seemed preoccupied with counting carbs, food exchanges, exercise, and compliance with medications. By the turn of the new century, diabetics were scolded for being overweight and lazy. People were getting fat and inactive. Children were becoming obese. While I had gained the classic "truncal obesity" around my midsection, I never considered myself fat. I certainly didn't have poor eating habits. I rarely snacked and hardly ever ate dessert. I've come to the conclusion that being overweight is the result of diabetes, not the cause. After all, if extra weight caused diabetes, every fat person would be diabetic. They're not.

Another part of the equation was the belief that diabetics lie and cheat on their diets. Almost every health-care worker I've encountered seems to expect that diabetics won't be honest in reporting their diets and their exercise. The truth for myself is that I can do everything exactly the same. But one day, my readings will run high and the next day low. Just when I think that I've discovered an answer to the diabetic riddle, I'm confounded by the inability to duplicate the end results. My experience leads me to believe that diabetes is mostly a stress-driven disease. My numbers go up when my anxiety level increases and my ability to effect positive change is stymied. I also think that individuals with diabetes must find a balance on their own.

By the next year, I reluctantly called to make an appointment with my female doctor. I was overjoyed to hear that she was taking a leave of absence for a while, and I'd have to see someone else. I was delighted to switch to Dr. M., whom I'd heard good things about. He at least was good at writing my prescriptions, and he didn't question my reliance on natural remedies.

It helps that I seem to possess a high level of magical thinking. I refuse to accept the notion that diabetes is chronic and progressive. I really believe that there's a formula for each diabetic to achieve good blood sugar numbers. I continuously try new combinations of things to help my diabetes. I had high hopes for my coyote melon. I took a piece of it almost every day, sucking on the dried particle of root. My numbers seemed to be improving. And finally, I came to the last piece in the jar that Carlos had given to me in Mexico.

* * *

It was February 2001 and I needed to resupply my coyote melon. I did a search on the computer, putting in "melon de coyote." Nothing came up. I looked in herbal books and at Mexican markets. Nothing. One day, I was talking to a patient/friend. He had owned a greenhouse and knew a lot about botany. He suggested that I try my search using the English, "coyote melon." Bingo, there was some information about the plant. A woman wrote a book about healing plants and had two pages devoted to coyote melon. I bought the book from Amazon. I also found an herb company that sent pickers into the wild to fetch specific medicinal herbs. They were going to look for coyote melon for me in southern Colorado and New Mexico.

A month later, I was excited to learn that the herb company found my melon root. I agreed on a price and had them ship the entire root to me. I tried it and realized that it was poisonous. It was much more bitter than what I was used to. Even a small amount of it caused me to retch. The book mentioned that the plant was prone to mutation and could become poisonous. I finally decided that I was going to have to revisit Carlos. He and I could go into the desert and dig up some authentic plants.

I called Carlos and told him what I was planning. I used my frequent-flyer miles and a time-share trade to go back to Los Cabos and visit him. I planned ahead because I was sure that customs would not want me bringing in exotic plants from Mexico. I packed two suitcases, one for my clothes and the other with some gifts for Carlos and his wife and children. There would be plenty of room to bring back my treasure. Just before leaving Minneapolis, a patient came to see me, who was a taxidermist. I mentioned my anticipated problem with customs.

He gave me his card and said, "Dave, if customs confiscate your plants, give them this card, and they can ship the plants directly to me in Burnsville, and I'll release them back to you." This man had a license to bring in any flora or fauna from all parts of the world.

I still thought of my adventure as if it was a *Mission: Impossible* episode. Carlos met me at the airport and brought me to his house, where his wife fixed a light dinner. I met his entire family and his niece. Then I went to my hotel. Carlos was going to pick me up in a few days, and we were going to find coyote melon. I told him that I wanted to see how it grew and to get roots and seeds to try and grow it back in Minneapolis. Carlos made it sound as if it was going to be a real adventure. In the end, we found all the melon I wanted right in the backyard of Carlos, under his mango trees. We celebrated with beer, and I paid Carlos two hundred dollars, which he had said earlier not to worry about but later asked for, for "the children."

I got on the plane and was scheduled to go through customs in Dallas. Carlos reassured me that the guard dogs wouldn't be alerted by the smell of the roots. I checked my bag with thirty pounds of roots and had to reclaim it to go through customs. I bought a few tourist things so that I'd have something to declare. I handled the heavy luggage as if it was featherlight. I was at the head of the line and had a choice of agents to approach. I chose the young blonde woman and smiled a lot at her. Her concern was whether I was bringing in Cuban cigars. I told her that I didn't smoke, and she waved me through. Mission accomplished.

Once home, I showed Art my treasure. Then I photographed the roots and tried to rehydrate some of them. None of them came back to life. I had several seedpods, which I opened, and I was able to sprout some of the seeds and grow little plants. I also found a nursery in Tucson, which carried my coyote melon plants, and I ordered four of them. The rest of the roots I cut into thick chips and dried them. After they dried, I put the pieces into airtight jars. I've enough roots to last me the rest of my life and to experiment with anyone else that may want to try it.

Chapter Twenty-Seven

The Big Five-O

In 2001, I was going to have a milestone birthday. July 1, I would turn fifty. It seemed unreal to me. I felt like I was about thirty-four. Except, of course, that now I had adult-onset diabetes. After a year of experimenting and with my numbers under control and my use of oral medications and my root, I felt like I at least had a handle on diabetes. I was still annoyed that the medical community was not doing more about things like supplements, spices and natural herbs, and optimal food combinations. My blood sugar numbers remained fairly stable.

* * *

Sometime during the winter of 2001, Esther fell and broke her hip. I knew that this wasn't a good sign and can often lead to various other health problems. She was in a nursing home for her birthday in March for rehabilitation. Now that I wasn't teaching anymore, I decided to buy her a small gift and go visit her since she was at Redeemer, just a few blocks from my office.

She was so thrilled to see me and she kept saying, "No one is going to believe me if I tell them that my doctor came to visit me."

Despite her broken hip, she looked good. She also mended swiftly and was only at the nursing home for a couple of weeks.

She resumed her visits to my office; but since most of her drivers had, by then, predeceased her, she was now taking a cab. After a few visits by cab, I was waiting for the cab driver to pick her up and take her home, when I offered to drive her home myself rather than wait for the cab. Once I took her home the first time, the next time she made her appointment, she asked if I could pick her up and take her back home. Of course, I agreed, and she added two dollars to her payment each visit. This became our tradition for the next few years.

* * *

After my father died, I seemed to have much more time in my life. Art and I had been planning to finish a remodel on his house. When Dad and Jeanne were living with us, everything was on hold. Our second bedroom was piled with tools and odds and ends that we needed in order to finish the kitchen. We even had a brand new dishwasher sitting in its box in the living room. We used the box as a high table to stack things on. The plan was for Art and me to work jointly on the kitchen. It soon became clear that I'd get more accomplished and be much faster if I did most of the work myself. Art was more helpful at funding the project.

Our kitchen was small and inefficiently laid out. The old refrigerator used to sit in the back hallway. Art had purchased a new refrigerator, but of course, it didn't fit in the space the old one had occupied. The entire east wall of the kitchen was floor-to-ceiling custom maple cabinets. Sometime in the sixties, Sears came in and made horrible changes. They moved the only radiator that was under the windows and put it under the sink. Then they put a stainless steel sink and corner cabinet over the radiator. We had the hottest sink in the winter. The new refrigerator had nowhere to go but in front of the only windows in the kitchen.

My plan was to eliminate the middle row of cabinets on the east wall and cut the bottom row of cabinets to make a space for the refrigerator in the far corner. Then I wanted to put a window on the east wall where the cabinets had been. I also planned to move the radiator back to where it'd been previously, under the windows. I was hoping to reuse the cabinets I removed and use them above the sink and stove. Unfortunately, they didn't quite fit, and I decided to build my own new cabinets for the remaining space. The old stove was overly large. I figured that by replacing it with a normal-sized gas stove, I would have room to install a dishwasher. We'd been using an old portable dishwasher that finally broke down.

Since I was doing the work myself, I could stage it and do things little by little, with minimal disruption to our lives. The project took over a year. In the end, it only cost about four thousand dollars, which included a new stove and dishwasher and granite countertops.

The first thing we did was to move out the old stove and put a smaller new one in its place. We did this in the winter. The monster stove was really heavy. It took both of us, using all our strength to get it outside and down the back steps. We set it on the ground. Eventually, we were going to have to get it to the alley. I started to call various charities to donate a working gas stove. I didn't find any interest in gas. They only wanted electric stoves. Before I could find a home for the stove, we had a blizzard. The stove and pathway to the alley was now covered by two feet of snow.

I was beginning to think the stove would have to sit there all winter until the snow melted. Then I had a dream. Many of my problems seem to be solved in dreams. In the dream, I was skiing down a steep hill. I looked over my shoulder to see the stove skiing down behind me. Eureka! We had purchased two pair of old downhill skis from Goodwill a couple of years earlier, and they went unused in the fruit cellar. The next morning, I found the skis and put them under the stove and was easily able to slide the stove to the alley. I put a big sign on the stove saying, "Take me—I am free and I work." The stove was gone by the end of the day. Perfect recycling.

The following spring, Art and I discussed the possibility of adopting a child. We'd thought about this on-and-off for some time. I finally had a small sum of money from my inheritance, and we were both getting older. My thought was "now or never." After a search on the Internet and questions to some of my patients, I asked Art if he wanted to adopt a child or build a new garage. We both agreed that a child would change our lives so completely that we were better off enjoying other people's children occasionally. Art said he would rather have a garage.

Soon after that, I started cutting down a beautiful ash tree that was planted right under all the utility lines and in the way of the garage. I trimmed the branches away from the power lines. When I was ready to fell the tree, Art was there pulling on a rope. There was a small gap that I was hoping the tree would land in. This tree was over twenty feet tall and eighteen inches thick at the base. Timber! The tree fell, missed the gap, and landed on the power lines of the neighbor. Oops.

Fortunately, my brother Jim is an electrician. I made a call to him, and he came out to fix the mast that'd pulled off the neighbor's house. Our neighbor had started the process of selling her house so she wasn't terribly concerned.

When Jim was working on the mast, he said, "The mast must've been damaged before."

I admitted, "When I cut down the silver maple tree several years ago, the mast was pulled out, but my neighbor thought that it happened from a storm."

I started checking the city codes for garages. I found out that in order to build a big double-car garage, we were required to tear down our single-car garage. The rules and regulations were so contrary to our dreams that we gave up on the idea of a new garage. Instead, we decided to dig a pond. We bought a liner and started digging a twelve-by-six-foot pond by hand shovel. I dug most of it even though Art helped. We were fortunate that the ground was sandy and easy to dig. I wanted it deep so that if we put fish in it, the raccoons couldn't snack on them. It was over four feet deep in the center. I created a waterfall on the end, where I piled the dirt.

We've had the pond ever since. I bought some koi and several twelve-cent feeder goldfish and planted water lilies and other water plants in the pond. For a few years, we heated the pond all winter but stopped when Art looked at his electric bill and noticed it was costing over fifty dollars each month to heat it. Now I round up the fish and put them in a plastic kiddie pool in the basement for the winter along with the tropical water plants. All the koi died. I haven't replaced them. The goldfish breed every summer, and the population remains at around fifty.

In the meantime, home maintenance is a constant concern. Art's house had a broken cleanout at the sewer exit. He put a plastic bag over the hole, but the sewer gas eventually ate away the plastic. One day, I was doing laundry and the line backed up. I noticed that water was coming up from under the cement basement floor. After further inspection, I realized that the cast-iron pipe under the floor was leaking. Having little extra money, we decided to fix it ourselves. Over the Labor Day weekend, we rented a jackhammer and bought PVC pipes and a cleanout and proceeded to jackhammer the basement cement floor. Then we had to dig dirt away from the iron pipe. The worst part was cutting the pipe. We had little room to work in, and we took turns using a small hacksaw. It took hours, and we got filthy with dirt, sweat, and sewage. We took movie pictures of our progress. We were able to complete the work and fill the hole. I told Art that now was the time to bury anyone, if he was interested in seeing them disappear. We cemented the floor, and the sewer line was better than ever.

* * *

For my big birthday in 2001, I told Art that I wanted to go to the Canary Islands. He got excited about it too when I told him there was a clothing-optional ocean beach and a lot of gay nightclubs. I discovered a cheap charter flight that left from London and booked two tickets for our trip. Then I found a good-priced flight from Minneapolis to London round-trip. We booked the trip for the end of May, a little more than a month before my real birthday. I bleached my hair blond just for drama. I liked the look of a blond frosted head of hair. I was going to be fifty!

We got to London and realized that we had to travel an hour each way from the airport to our London hotel and then back to the airport to go to the Canary Islands. It cost thirty dollars each way for each of us. We stayed at a hotel in southwest London, which was "gay." The rooms were tiny. There was a bar in the basement that was home to some of the homeliest drag queens that we had ever laid eyes on. Our room was two floors up from the bar. It seemed as if everyone smoked in Europe, and the smoke from the bar traveled directly up to our room and made Art and me think that the hotel was on fire. The bartender was Scottish and told everyone else that we were Americans, so they should speak slowly to us. The Scot didn't have any olives for martinis. He carefully measured each drink to exact specification and told us that the authorities were strict with enforcing volume violators.

We didn't spend a lot of time at the hotel. We took the subway and saw many of the usual tourist attractions. We saw the Crown Jewels, Traitor's Gate, and The Tower of London. We ate fish and chips. We even went to the Tate Modern Museum. We had fun riding the subway. We found a little Spanish tapas restaurant and ate there a couple nights. Then we flew to the Canary Islands. We arrived at Grand Canaria. Our plane was much less roomy than the usual American planes. Everything on the plane was for sale. If one wanted a can of soda, it was a six-ounce size and cost a couple of dollars. All the flight attendants had mobile credit card machines strapped to their waists. The flight seemed to be endless.

When we arrived, we got a taxi and found our time-share hotel. It was well laid out and comfortable. Almost the entire building was filled with Germans. Many of the television stations were broadcasting in German. We found the nude beach. Of course, it was about as far as one could get from civilization. It required a three-mile hike through mountains of sand to get there. There were roped pathways to guide us. In the middle of this desert, there was an occasional oasis of trees and shrubs. Sometimes, there'd be naked men sunning themselves on the more obscure oasis edges.

Once, we tried putting a blanket down in a clump of trees. Within minutes, large lizards about two to three feet in length started approaching us. I wasn't sure if they wanted water, food, or us. I gave them some beer and hoped that they'd go away. I never knew if they'd bite, but I didn't want to find out. We only stayed about an hour in the trees and then went back. There were a lot of gay establishments in a nearby shopping mall back in town.

However, they didn't open for business until 11:00 PM and we often went to bed by 9:30 PM.

The gay beach was also a disappointment, and the water was cold even at the end of May. Many of the other guys were English and sort of prudish. It was a long way to go to see some ass. Our final day, we decided to stay near our time-share. We went to the pool and took a couple of chairs. We weren't there very long before a couple of big old topless German women came out to sun. One was livid and speaking in German.

She was ranting to her friend, "Der Blond (me) took my chair that I've had all week."

Of course, she didn't realize that I knew some German. There were two other German women lying topless in the sun, and one was trying very hard to get my sexual attention. She and her friend finally left the pool in defeat. I finally tried to take a swim in the pool and immediately found out it was unheated and freezing cold. The Germans thought it resembled Hawaii, but for me, it seemed more like the North Sea. We had a terrible time finding the bus stop when we were leaving to go to the airport. At the last minute, we found out we were on the wrong side of a large busy intersection. We darted through heavy traffic carrying all of our luggage. They wouldn't store anything back in London even though we were booked to return. I was afraid that Art was going to have a heart attack.

Back in London, we felt more confident with the subway and did some more exploring. We made it to The British Museum and saw all the Egyptian artifacts that the English stole from Egypt. There was also a special exhibit on Cleopatra. It seemed to me that civilization waxed and waned several times before we got to where we are today. We thoroughly enjoyed our short time in London.

When we returned to Minneapolis, I had to get back to work, and I looked forward to telling Esther about all of our adventures. Fifty was looming just in the next month. I have to admit that I was a little preoccupied with the thought of that milestone. I loved my body and felt as though I had good reason to appreciate it. I was miffed about the diabetes, but I was beginning to learn to live with it. I felt so confident about my ability to manage it that when my insurance was up by July 1, I dropped my coverage. I found that I could buy my drugs in Canada through the Internet and save even more money.

Chapter Twenty-Eight

9/11

George Bush Jr. was a dumb jock. He smiled a lot and had trouble pronouncing nuclear. He'd only been in office a little less than a year. Already, I realized that he was the dumbest president that I'd lived under to this point. Esther didn't like him either. Once, she told me that she'd willingly shoot him.

She said to me one day, "I wish I could shoot him. After all, they couldn't put an old lady like me in jail too long."

I cautioned her, "I don't think you should say that to too many people." Then I added, "I'm sure you would have a hard time getting close to that guy." I wondered if she had ever fired a gun.

Esther had all her savings in Putnam funds. I'd begun to invest for my own retirement in mutual funds. In fact, when Dad died, all of us children got a small amount of his stock, and I added that to my investments in the stock market. Through 2000, stocks were still growing at a fast pace.

By early 2001, the stock market started pulling back. Esther said that her money manager wanted her to sell her Putnam stock. Then, on September 11, 2001, I was getting ready for work and had the usual morning news on. They were reporting about a plane crashing into one of the World Trade Center buildings. I didn't pay much attention, thinking that a small commuter plane had strayed off course and accidentally crashed. Then as I was watching the television screen, I saw a big jumbo jet crash right into the second World Trade building. It was a completely confusing scene. Right away, I thought that this was some terrible plot. When I got to work,

I turned on the news from my computer. One of my favorite patients, Nelson, came in for a massage. He and I couldn't believe what we were hearing. I muddled through the massage while we both kept our ear to the computer. Of course, there was also the crash at the Pentagon and in Pennsylvania.

The response that followed was eerie. Art and I live under a flight path in and out of MSP airport. That night, and a few nights after that, there wasn't any noise from traffic going in or out of the airport. People were in shock. I don't think anyone expected that the two World Trade Towers would collapse. It was hard to comprehend that thousands of people died along with the passengers in the aircraft. The scope of the whole plot was beyond everyone's wildest nightmares.

There was an immediate attempt to protect our president, and within hours, Bush had decided to "go to war" over the incident. I couldn't believe that without knowing who the real enemy was, we can so quickly declare war. It seemed to me that such a war could never be won. News coverage, as one would expect, was constant, repetitious, and dripping with sensationalism. Every day, I'd get the paper on the front step and hope that it was all a bad dream. While the actions that had concluded were daunting, I didn't see how a declaration of war was going to help matters. In my mind, the terrorists had finally gotten lucky and succeeded. It wasn't likely to happen again, at least on such a massive level.

After 9/11, I finally realized that most Americans were isolated and totally insecure with themselves. The level of fear was more apparent as the days went on. To confound the issues, Bush decided that he had unfinished business with Saddam in Iraq. The administration started a rumor that tied Saddam not only to 9/11 but also to weapons of mass destruction. It became obvious that Bush wanted to dethrone the same man America had put into power thirty years earlier. We were going to fight the "evildoers" of the world, and Bush was going to tell us who they were.

Art and I sat and listened to the buildup against Saddam and tried to be realistic. Bush was giving Saddam no options. According to Bush, Saddam obviously had nuclear weapons, and we were going to invade his country if he didn't produce them. Having majored in International Relations at the U of MN, it was clear to me that we were going to war with Iraq to placate the insecurity that welled up in America over terrorism. Saddam wasn't a nice guy, but that doesn't mean we should kill ten times as many people as he did so we can put a new government of our choosing into power. It was a thinly veiled attempt to get control over Iraqi oil. It would also make Cheney's faltering Halliburton several billion dollars.

I also couldn't believe that Bush went on to belittle our previous world friends by using extortion to try to build a coalition among them and against Saddam. It was all so ill conceived and Wild West. And then, I realized that the terrorist had indeed won when traveling by air was permanently altered to include so much fake posturing and inconveniencing of everyone by the TSA.

The terrorist would not have succeeded if the airlines weren't so greedy that they took cash for quick one-way first-class tickets and asked no questions. In Minnesota, we were at least alert enough to recognize that an unskilled Arab man who wanted to take flying lessons to learn how to steer a jumbo jet might be suspicious. The FBI was alerted and Moussaui was arrested. But so few people were using common sense. It wasn't helpful that the government deliberately ramped up the fear level.

I was angry with 9/11 and also angry that our government chose such a stupid response. I also had a difficult time trying to understand why people were so slow to resume a normal life. In the next few months, the stock market plummeted. I lost, as did most Americans, almost half of what I had in there. People had so little disposable income that they stopped putting their money into things they deemed luxuries, including massage and out-of-pocket chiropractic.

I'd built my business model under Clinton. I offered good service at a reasonable price. But now, with a cash shortage, people were patronizing offices that took insurance even when the service was overpriced and of dubious quality. On top of all that, my patient base of gay men and lesbians was coming up short with money. Others were moving out of state, and some were dying of HIV. Fortunately,

I'd cut my expenses to the bone and had very little overhead. Many of my regulars were still coming in, including Esther, but they were coming in less often.

* * *

Art and I continued to go to St. Martin each year and also spent some time at Breezy Point. We also went to Palm Springs but spent only a few days rather than a full week. Travel by plane was now a real chore and was never the fun that it used to be before 9/11. Airlines were cutting back on service even before 9/11. Then gas prices began rising. Fuel was unpredictable for drivers and airlines alike, and it resulted in severe cost cutting. Flying became much less pleasant.

Meals were phased out beginning in 1999. Some airlines offered them after that, but it was rare to find meals on most airlines after 2002. Once, Art and I were flying to St. Martin. It's a long flight with at least one stop. We bought some really good prepared salads for our flight and brought them onboard. Well into the flight, after the beverage cart rolled through, we took out our salads. We were the envy of most of the folks sitting nearby.

Some of them asked, "Where did you get such beautiful salads?"

I responded, "Just ask a flight attendant. Tell them you're diabetic and need to have a snack." I added, "There's actually plenty of food in the back. You should demand to have some of it."

The flight attendants weren't very happy with me for alluding to food on a nonservice flight.

Another time, we were using frequent-flyer miles to fly to Palm Springs. It was during a merger of US Airways and America West. We arrived in Palm Springs without incident.

When we got to the airport to return, one of the workers at the counter said to us, "I can only get you to Phoenix today."

I asked, "What is the problem?"

She replied, "Your return flight from Phoenix to Minneapolis no longer exists." She began to put tags on our luggage that said Phoenix.

I said, "That's unacceptable."

She threw up her hands and walked away.

Her cohort, a young man, said, "I'll see what I can do to help. Take a seat and I'll try to help you."

Art explained to the man, "He's a doctor, and he's got to be back in Minneapolis by 8:00 AM tomorrow."

We sat and waited.

Over a half hour later, the man approached us and said, "A driver will drive you to LAX, two and a half hours away. Then you'll board the red-eye Northwest jet and be in Minneapolis by 6:00 AM."

This seemed to be the only solution. So a driver picked us up in a van, and he drove us to Los Angeles. When we got there, we got our tickets and proceeded to security. I never gave it any thought, but we were both detained by security and taken separately to a holding area. We were questioned along with a thorough search and pat down. It turned out that now we were suspect because we had one-way, last-minute, expensive cash tickets from an airport that we never flew into. I was tired and weak from hunger and wanted to protest. I felt like we were in Nazi Germany. Yet I knew that protest would only make matters worse.

We finally got a bite to eat and boarded our plane, which was set to depart at twelve thirty in the early morning. At 2:00 AM, we had yet to move an inch, and we kept getting reports from the pilot that something was broken but they were working on it. At 2:30 AM, we were all told to leave the airplane and go to a different gate, where an identical plane was being readied. I've never seen so many dejected people. Everyone knew that they weren't going to make their business meetings or flight connections. We boarded the second plane and waited for the gangway to close so we could finally take off. That wasn't going to happen either. There were problems with this plane as well. Being claustrophobic, I got off the plane and tried to go to a restroom. They were all closed for cleaning. There were neither vending machines nor food services open. I asked the gate attendant if we should be considering rebooking on a flight leaving at 6:00 AM. He assured us that one plane or another would be fixed before then. He asked that I return to the plane and wait. Then at 4:30 AM, an announcement was made that the flight had been cancelled, and everyone needed to rebook. There was a mad dash to try for the 6:00 AM plane. After that, the next plane would be leaving at 8:00 AM. There was one line of over a hundred people, and only one poor woman trying to change all the tickets. Luckily, we got the last two seats available on the 6:00 AM plane.

We've had other terrible flights since 9/11 but probably none as bad as that one.

* * *

In the early years of 2000, Art and I tried to rekindle our love life. Since I was diagnosed as diabetic, I began more often to assume the role of a bottom. It was getting more difficult for me to maintain an erection than it used to be. We both quit smoking a few years earlier, and both of us gained some weight. Art gained a little more than I did. Then Art also found out he was diabetic. We kept things from getting too stale by watching porn movies. DVD was emerging as the new format. Art bought me leather chaps and other gear to enhance our sexual experiences. We purchased a sling and even bought two penis pumps. Then Viagra became a need-to-have drug for good sex. We tried a lot of stuff and got bored with almost all of it eventually. We started to have sex less frequently.

Occasionally, I'd ask different close patients about their sexual frequency, and I heard a lot of the same things. Gay or straight, frequency of sex between partners usually seems to diminish over time. I didn't like hearing that. At the same time, there was more and more sexual content on the World Wide Web. Some of it had to be purchased, but a surprising amount was free. We had a computer at home, and I had a computer at my office. To further confound our relationship, the computer was more or less a solo experience.

I found myself going online to various Web sites whenever it was slow at work. Art would come home from work and go on the computer. He was sometimes on it for several hours because most sites he wanted to access were not allowed where he worked. Art would tell me about Web sites, and I would look at them when I got to my office. Our early favorite was barebackcity.com. Gay.com was also a good site. There were many others.

The interesting thing about the computer is that you can be anyone that you want to be when you are online. You can post pictures and stats that you make up. The pictures don't have to be you. They can be someone that you aspire to be or fantasize about being. You can make up anything that you want. Of course, everyone else is doing the same thing. It's often a total break from reality. Now that I was over fifty, it was even more important for me to be a healthy, virile, young-looking, sensual gay male. It was just as important that other gay men see me as that handsome want-to-have-sex-with kind of guy.

* * *

I knew that Esther wasn't interested in my sex life. To her, I was a good friend and faithful doctor. When Esther broke her hip, I felt terrible about it. Later that spring, Esther started asking me if I could take her and her son Charles to Eden Prairie so that she could buy a phone with an amplifier. She was becoming hearing impaired, and it was difficult for her to use an ordinary phone. Charles didn't have a car and didn't drive. I knew it would cost a fortune for them to go there by cab. I finally told Esther that, of course, I would take them, but it would have to be on a Wednesday. We made arrangements and I drove them to get a new phone.

Once there, the staff asked, "Are you a son or grandson?"

I answered, "No, Esther is my patient and I am her chiropractor."

They were surprised to hear it. We left with a perfect phone for Esther.

* * *

Esther always made me feel good. She was complimentary toward my vocation, skill, and accomplishments. She was very nonjudgmental, and I later realized that she was one of the only people in my life that seemed to love me unconditionally. I was candid with her when it came to my chiropractic business. Since Bush II, my revenue stream had become a trickle. As a sensitive and caring doctor, I often took it personally when fewer patients came in to see me and my bills mounted. I'd cut my expenses to the bone, and I still wasn't able to come up with the small sums of money that I needed to keep current on my bills.

I didn't want to admit to being a failure, especially to Art. He was secure in a government office job with precise hours and pay schedules. He got paid vacations and sick leave and had a growing pension. I struggled to get from one bill to the next. When it came to vacations and time off, I had to use my credit cards. At least the credit card companies were generously increasing my lines of credit. I was paying for my medications over the Internet and getting them from Canada. Now that I didn't have to pay health insurance premiums, I could use that money to buy drugs. Business continued to slow.

Fortunately, I had a lot of home projects that kept me busy. When Art and I went to the State Fair that fall, I had a new credit card with a line of credit burning a hole in my pocket. As always, we stopped to see the hot tub display. I was nearly talked into a spa when the salesman got distracted and Art pulled me away from the booth. I continued dreaming about a spa and how it would be good for us with our diabetes. I talked to patients to find out which spa was preferred in Minnesota's climate. Within a month, we were out in our yard, trying to figure out where to put the spa. After laying a foundation, I went and purchased a new spa for Art's birthday and Christmas and all future big-gift holidays.

We both had fantasies about having sexual adventures in a hot tub. After we started using it, we realized that one gets so relaxed that it isn't very convenient to have sex in a hot tub. We enjoyed the therapeutic aspects of it even though sex wasn't usually a part of the experience. Sometimes it was a good warm-up however.

When my work was busy and I made enough money to cover my bills, I was deeply satisfied. When I went in to the office and the phone didn't ring, I was scared. It wasn't supposed to be this way. I had hopes of being retired at fifty and only working because I enjoyed the work. The lack of business was crushing my ego. I was taking it personally even though when patients finally came back for treatment after a long absence, the reason for their scarcity was almost always a case of things going on in their own lives, not a reflection of my skill.

Art is older than I, and he's less preoccupied with his libido than I am. The hot tub wasn't improving things very much. Sitting alone in my office, waiting for the next patient, I began going to Web sites that offered some degree of sexual titillation. I'm not the most knowledgeable computer user. Even today, I have dial-up service. I began going to sites that were nationwide. In the early stages, I accessed sites where I could read profiles or see pictures. Eventually, I learned ways to use the microphone and speakers to have picture and sound capabilities. Usually, I would use those features on the home computer, where we had high-speed cable. I even purchased a camera for the home computer.

I was often far behind the technology that took me to some Web sites. I remember going to one site, and suddenly, I was talking to a supposed nineteen-year-old guy in Ohio. He was role-playing and wanted me to join him. He described a scene where he was at a football stadium, and he went below the bleachers and wanted to meet an older man like myself that he could have sex with. I attempted to play out my role, and he kept correcting me and asking me to call his cock a penis.

It was such a funny way to have safe sex that I kept up the pretense until he shouted, "I'm cumming!"

By the time I got back to that Web site a week or so later, I'd already forgotten how to get onto the site.

Every Web site seemed to have a slightly different variation of interaction. For a while, I got into gay.com. Initially, I looked at pictures and read the profiles. I was careful to go to rooms that were not local. It was easy to talk to anyone online by typing him or her messages. I worked on my own profile and pictures. I found some flattering nude photos of myself. I was gradually becoming quite adept at interacting with many different guys. Bareback City changed their Web site because of threats from the Bush administration. Some of the other sites made access more difficult or eliminated the free features. In the beginning, I paid to be on gay.com, but when my membership was terminated, I didn't renew it.

Chapter Twenty-Nine

The Perfect Storm

In 2002, Art and I were in St. Martin again midwinter. For several years, Art had been suggesting that we have a more committed relationship. After knowing each other fifteen years, I, too, wanted something more solid. I'd recently gotten another new credit card, which was making me itchy to spend money in The West Indies. We went to Phillipsburg, and I convinced Art to enter a jewelry store. It was Little Switzerland, and we'd been there a few times previously.

I went to the case that contained men's rings. There was a series of rings in different gemstones all set in channel settings. I was drawn to an emerald ring. There was also a ruby and sapphire version of the same ring. I tried on the emerald and then decided to try the ruby.

I asked Art, "Do any of these rings look good to you?"

He said, "The sapphire ring is beautiful."

We talked, and I said to him, "I am willing to buy each of us a ring as a commitment to you and to our relationship."

After a typical back-and-forth bargaining with the saleswoman, I bought a ruby ring with diamonds and a matching sapphire ring with diamonds. Ruby is my birthstone and sapphire is Art's. The sales woman sent the rings to the jeweler to be resized. After strolling Front Street, we circled back to pick up our rings.

At The View, I got down on my knees and asked Art to be my partner for life. I think he was ready to cry. Of course, gay people were not allowed the possibility of marriage at this time. Also, without marriage, there isn't much social pressure for monogamy.

We continued a nice vacation and proudly wore our rings home to Minneapolis.

* * *

Once home, the storm started brewing. Idleness can be the devil's playground. The worst thing for a sole proprietor is lack of business. I went to the office each day, ready for an onslaught of patients. Sometimes, the phone didn't even ring all day. Other days, it rang, and a telemarketer was there to try to take any money you might have made that week. Scammers were all over with offers to put you in the who's who list of America if you just paid them for a membership first. Yellow pages other than the real Yellow Pages Directory wanted to list you on the Internet and in the book they published. But these offers weren't legitimate. The Police Federation called for a donation. Even The Better Business Bureau had selected me and would feature my name to its members for a small fee of six hundred dollars per year. My already fragile ego began to crash, and my pride prevented me from telling anyone. Esther knew about it because I remained honest with her.

I know that I'm a good chiropractor. However, one begins to question why patients aren't coming back. I began to use my magical thinking. I filed my cards, not by alphabet but by most recent patient, on the top of a big stack. I liked to play a game where I would go through a number of cards and think hard about each name on a card. Sometimes I went deep into the pile and put old cards on the top. Oddly, the people that I put my mind to often called within one or two days of channeling them. Once I went deep in the pile and found a card of someone who'd only come in one time a couple of years earlier. I couldn't remember him, so I actually went to his chart to try to get a better idea of who he was. On his card, I'd written a note that he was going to be moving soon after his first visit. I finally recalled who the man was. The very next day, Jeff called.

He said, "You probably don't remember, me but I was in to see you a couple of years ago."

I answered, "Hello, Jeff. I wondered how your move went and I've been thinking about you."

He answered, "Wow, you have a really good memory. I love where I am living now, and I finally need to make an appointment for an adjustment."

Business came and went in spurts. Then there were cancellations. It was very defeating when I saw on caller ID that I'd missed a potential patient, and they didn't call back. Once in a while, I'd be so busy that it was difficult for me to run the entire office alone. But most of the time, I had lots of holes in my schedule. That's when I would turn on my computer.

* * *

By 2002, in the fall, I started going to local rooms and chatting with guys who lived in the Twin Cities. I enjoyed typing back and forth and learning about different relationships and sexual appetites. I'm not really sure why, but I was often drawn into conversation with people that had what I consider bizarre fetishes. When I had an opportunity to make computer chat, I enjoyed daring myself to talk to people with different ideas about kinky sex. I wanted to look at everything, imaginable or not, that I could discover on the Internet.

For most of 2002, I was content with just looking at various Web sites and occasionally chatting in rooms where my identity was protected. When one revisits rooms, one begins to see the patterns of individuals and what they like to talk about and how often they show up. It was an easy stumble to go from chatting to actually meeting up with someone. What I unwittingly met up against while using the computer was intermittent rewards. Out of ten or twenty attempts to meet someone, maybe two or three people would carry things through to an actual meeting. And then of those two or three, either one or maybe none of them would actually be a pleasant experience. What I wasn't aware of was the fact that the inconsistent rewards were conditioning my behavior to make me try harder. Through a weird marriage of behavioral modification and technology addiction, I was becoming addicted to online sex.

Another operating factor was that once there was an encounter, the rules of anonymity precluded any further contact with the person that was met. Anonymous one-time encounters were the standard. It was very confusing and a huge waste of time, most of the time. My first attempts to make contact were safe, and condoms were always used except for oral sex. I discovered that I was allergic to latex condoms. I'd usually get rashes if I wore them or rashes if I was penetrated with them. I knew that there were polyurethane condoms, but they, of course, were more expensive and less readily available.

During these times, I was also going to Aliveness Project to do my volunteer service of free chiropractic. I'd talk to the (mostly) guys and learn about their sexual needs and how they met them. I began to blur the distinctions between viral positive and negative. When I was a smoker and I quit, I often sided with smokers for having a right to smoke somewhere else besides the outdoors when it's thirty below zero. In Palm Springs, Art would look at other guests sharing our guesthouse and quietly note how skinny some of them were. He cautioned me that sex with skinny guys should always be avoided. My feelings were that if one wants to have sex with a stranger, one should take precautions as if they were positive and eliminate any fear of contracting anything from them.

Another thing was happening at the same time. The message of safe sex had bombarded the gay and lesbian community incessantly for twenty years. It was starting to get old, and I was becoming resistant to the message. I came out during the days of hippies and free love. Now spontaneity was something only long-term partners could have, only if they were faithful to each other. Many of the sexual messages coming from the mainstream suggested that once one had been infected with the virus, sex shouldn't be considered again. For me, it was very much a case of message fatigue.

The whole idea of safe sex being on a scale of more safe to less safe was difficult to convey. All the rules were based on fear of the unknown and almost dared fearless people, like me, to try to test the boundaries. Most positive guys that I worked with who had negative partners told me the only time they used condoms was when the positive partner penetrated the negative one anally. I started to rationalize that if I was healthy enough, even unprotected anal intercourse with someone positive wasn't likely to transmit the virus.

I thought that it was a terrible message for people who'd gotten infected to hear that they should now be abstinent. It seemed especially harsh because there was some progress being made in treatment. Positive people were still dying but at a much slower rate than just five years before. Some guys played around without telling their temporary partners their infection status. For me that was scary. However, it takes two to spread the virus, and there should be an insistence by at least one person to make the sex safe. There are also many guys who aren't aware of their status because they don't test.

I'm very good at rationalization. I've always been. I heard from somewhere that if a person has unsafe penetration from an HIV-infected individual, only one in a hundred times will the virus be transferred successfully. What I turned a blind eye to was that it only takes one successful exposure to have HIV forever. I'd become too comfortable with the virus. I don't like to let fear govern my life. But I was trying to rationalize my irrational desire to have bareback sex with men. I could still remember how fulfilling spontaneous sex used to be. I had it with Art. We always had wonderful sex together. But Art alone couldn't keep my ego from being crushed.

The perfect storm that was brewing around me was encouraging me to dismiss the wise precautions of safe sex. It didn't have anything to do with Art. It had to do with my need to feel strong and youthful and virile and adequate. I was over fifty, and my business was failing in spite of the fact that I knew that I was a good chiropractor. I had too much time with nothing to do. I also yearned for the approval that my parents never really gave me. The computer was there, and occasionally, I got lucky and connected and got rewarded.

* * *

By the end of 2002, I'd mastered the computer enough to be able to chat and make connections online if I so desired. In December of that year, I received a call that brought an ex-friend back into my life.

Kevin was the guy that I moved to Boston for in 1975. We lived together there and had a lot of fun, and of course, we had great sex. After about a year of living with each other in Boston, I made a decision to disconnect with Kevin. I'd shared my first LSD experiences with him. Kevin was my first love. He was extremely handsome and could've easily been a model except for his small stature. He was a little vain and spent a lot of time looking into mirrors and buying face creams. He wasn't always fully forthcoming with me. Since that time in Boston, he was diagnosed as being schizophrenic. We kept in touch after I moved back to Minneapolis.

* * *

In 1982, Kevin was in Minnesota to visit his family. He called me and asked if I'd meet him and take him to the airport on his way out of town. I agreed, and I picked him up at the bus station, where he'd come from Hastings. It was New Years Eve. Kevin's plane was scheduled to take off around 9:00 PM. We sat around and talked, and after a short time, Kevin began to talk very irrationally. He went from somewhat normal to hearing voices and being very agitated. I was living with Darren, my boyfriend at that time. Darren had friends who worked at HCMC in the psych ward. Together, we agreed that Kevin wouldn't be able to board a plane in his condition. I had no choice but to take him to the hospital and have him admitted.

When I called his mother in Hastings, she blasted me and said, "What did you do to him? He was perfectly normal when he left here."

I felt terrible, as though I got beat up for doing the right thing. That was my New Year's gift for 1983.

Over the years, Kevin called occasionally. Usually, it was with a request for money. Of course, I didn't have enough money for myself, let alone for him to buy cigarettes with. But we talked maybe once or twice a year. He'd become a street person living in Los Angeles. It was sad for me, and I wished that I could help him, but I didn't have any resources to be generous to him. Then around Christmas 2002, I got a call from Kevin. Both the tone and the topic were so uncharacteristic of him. I saw from my caller ID that he was calling from Abbott Northwestern Hospital. Instead of asking me for favors, he posed questions to me.

He asked me, "Are you happy with your life? Are you satisfied with where you are in life?"

It wasn't a long conversation, and when I hung up, I noted that it was the most peculiar conversation that I'd ever had with Kevin. He seemed to be questioning his own existence.

* * *

By 2003, I felt an emptiness that I couldn't explain. My parents were both dead, and my business was stagnant. Art seemed more remote, and our sexual timing seemed to be more off than on. When we had time together, Art spent a lot of time on the computer.

At one point, I said to him, "I think you're addicted to the computer."

He bristled at that. I felt more alone. At the office, I went to more local gay men's Web sites. I slowly started getting more and more involved with sex and the computer.

Chapter Thirty

A Brewing Storm Continues

I don't remember exactly when my first actual face-to-face encounter with a stranger from the Internet occurred. What I do remember is that I felt compelled to venture deeper and deeper into this world of computer sex. The computer offered me inconsistent rewards. I didn't know it at the time, but I think I was slowly and deliberately having my behavior modified through classic B.F. Skinner behavioral techniques mixing up with new technology. Skinner experimented in the 1940s with the effectiveness of intermittent rewards and their role in promoting addiction. For me, inconsistent rewards of computer sex were equally addictive.

I felt that I'd stumbled into the rabbit's hole, and I was entering wonderland just as Alice had. When I first met up with an actual person from the computer, it seemed as though I was in a trance. The event was dreamlike, and I felt nervous and was almost shaking with anxiety. I had fear and trepidation. I actually went to houses of strangers and knocked on doors. I often parked blocks away. I usually left a piece of paper with a phone or address on it just in case the stranger was a lunatic and decided to murder me. With the paper, the police would have something to go on. At first, the sexual part was safe, and I used protection. I'd bring condoms or use theirs. What went on was usually already established with the computer chat. Sometimes, after 2002, I began to skip the protection offered by condoms. The immediate reward was more spontaneity and heightened sensation. I didn't think about the fact that I was now endangering Art and myself.

Along the sexual roadway, there were many failed attempts and a lot of wasted time. Of course, time is what I had most of then. Once I drove twenty miles to meet a guy in a red pickup so that we could have sex. The plan was to meet in a parking lot and then go to his house. On the way to the parking lot, I wondered which red pickup would be the one with my computer date inside. Once there, I realized that it was a very big lot. There weren't any red pickups nearby. I waited twenty minutes. I drove back to my computer, and I sent an angry e-mail to the guy. He replied that his boyfriend came home unexpectedly, and he was unable to keep the rendezvous.

Another time, I drove at least fifteen miles to a strange house in the northern suburbs to meet a younger man. When I knocked and rang the bell, no one answered. I was sure that someone was inside. I didn't know if I was given a bogus address or if someone inside didn't like my looks or … almost anything. But then, once in a while things worked out better.

Once, Art and I both took Viagra, and I sat down at our home computer. I found someone online who wanted to come over and play. With Art's consent, I invited the guy over. I wondered how much Art would want to participate in computer sex games. I played with the guy, but Art wasn't attracted to him. Art didn't really get excited the same way that I did. I admired Art's integrity.

The rewards from the computer were usually inconsistent. Only occasionally would I meet a really hot guy who was versatile, virile, and really fun to play with. Toward the end of 2003, I met enough guys online who played occasionally. We were sometimes able to get groups of four or five guys together at a time. I also decided to throw caution to the wind and begin playing without any protection. I rationalized my behavior by picking out half-truths about the HIV virus that made my risky behavior explainable in my mind. As a chiropractor, I've never bought the whole idea that contact with an organism was all that it takes to get infected. Most of the time, bacteria and viruses surround us, and it's our own weakness that permits these bad organisms access into our bodies. I was playing Russian roulette. I was also diabetic, so I was prone to bleeding gums and breaks in delicate tissues.

I felt uncomfortable about nagging Art to have more sex. I came to feel that I wasn't able to ask for sex from Art. I also was ashamed because I was having outside sex. Usually, I had to wait for Art to initiate sex. My being poor and feeling dependent on Art financially only contributed to my perception of being powerless in our relationship. It wasn't Art's fault. After being together so many years, sex between us lost some of its excitement. During my Viagra period, I'd sometimes pop a pill with the hope of having good sex, only to find that Art was on a totally different page when he arrived home from work. For him at that moment, the last thing that he wanted was sex. I also began to believe that erectile-dysfunction drugs created an irritability in me, which easily displaced the romantic warmth necessary for me to enjoy sex.

I never felt very much guilt about my escapades. I usually tried to play when Art was at work or out of town and when my business was slow or on my day off. I never had sex with patients. Sometimes, massage clients wanted to get frisky and complete their massage with a happy ending. I tried to screen most of that away from my office, when I got the first phone call from a prospective client. But some men seem to think that genitals are included when they hear full-body massage. I renamed my massage to call it therapeutic massage. I've had some awkward moments with a few clients. One of them stands out.

* * *

When he called for an appointment, I knew that he must've been responding to my ad in the local gay magazine, *Lavender.* It was the only place I advertised. When he arrived, he looked like a plump Mr. Clean—big with a baldhead. Once I started working on him, I saw that almost half of his body was tattooed. He also had a lot of body jewelry, including nipple rings and a Prince Albert in his penis. He refused the towel for a covering.

He kept saying things like, "Ooooh doctor, I love your strong hands!"

When it was time for him to roll over and lie on his back, his penis was fully erect. But in just a short time, he got on his hands and knees and presented his butt to my face.

He said, "I bet you find me irresistible. I bet you play with all your patients, and I want you to do anything you want with me. Please use my cock or ass any way you want."

I answered, "You need to settle down. I never do anything sexual with my patients. Unless you calm down, I can't continue your therapeutic massage."

I was getting grossed out because he had sores all over his body, and I thought that he might have tertiary syphilis.

He announce, "I deliver pizza, and I have sex with almost everyone I deliver pizza to." He added, "Everyone finds me irresistible."

I added, "It isn't a problem for me to resist you."

I also thought that he must be one of the slowest pizza delivery guys in town. He got back on his hands and knees and wagged his butt at me again. I stopped and told him his massage was over. I left the room. Then I wondered if he'd leave peaceably. Oddly, he'd paid in advance for his massage by credit card. He finally emerged from the massage room and looked sheepish.

He said on his way out, "Please don't say anything about this to my wife."

I couldn't believe it when two weeks later, this same guy called for an appointment for a massage.

I said, "I'm only going to give a therapeutic nonsexual massage."

He said, "I'll call again another time."

I responded, "Don't bother."

Similar things happened with much more attractive men. They'd sprout an erection and even start oozing from their penis. My usual response was to offer them some lubricant and leave the room for a moment. Sometimes, they'd indicate that they just wanted a good gluteal massage, and with that, I'd oblige them. But back on the Internet with an anonymous hookup, I wasn't constrained by convention.

It was usually the same series of clouds that opened up the downpour—slow business, lack of self-esteem, being unable to get fulfillment in my relationship, inconsistent rewards, my need to feel young and virile, and to be a healthy role model for my patients. I still equate good sexual performance with health. What I wanted most was someone, preferably a stranger, to really enjoy having sex with me.

* * *

I also felt bad when Art stopped wearing the sapphire ring that I'd given him after only a year. He developed a rash if he wore the ring continuously. I suggested he take it off overnight, but eventually, he put it away in a drawer. So in 2003, I was feeling even more alone, insecure, and unfulfilled. Art was more and more remote, and I was pulling away from him. Business was poor. The economy was bad. Bush was in power.

I was also sensing a deep loss that I couldn't explain. My first boyfriend Kevin's last words to me during the holidays of 2002, asking me if I was happy with my life, kept haunting me. In the meantime, I'd gotten better at using the Internet and sorting through my possibilities. I had fewer but mostly more rewarding encounters. I usually went to three different Web sites to make connections. I was naive about people on the Internet, who lie and make things up. I didn't know how vulnerable I was with my sinking self-esteem. Guys put up ads that say they're disease and drug free and want someone similar. Other guys post their age and conveniently leave off ten to fifteen years of their age and usually several pounds of their weight as well. Once in a while, I'd run into someone who was so depressed that they lived with months' worth of dirty dishes, empty pizza boxes, and rooms so packed with junk that one could barely navigate. That was disgusting.

It may sound as if I was a sexual maniac from what I have said so far. It wasn't quite that way. The number of encounters for me was far less than when I lived in Boston when I was twenty-three. I staggered my encounters to an occasional few, and I never planned anything in advance. It was whatever the circumstances allowed. Sometimes, I'd make plans because of a large hole in my work schedule, only to have a patient call needing some of that time. I'd always defer to the patient.

* * *

September of 2003, a mutual friend of my boyfriend Kevin, came to my office as a patient.

She asked me, "Did you hear about Kevin?"

I said, "No, I haven't heard from him since December."

Then in a solemn tone, she said, "Kevin committed suicide with an overdose of drugs on a beach in Los Angeles in March."

I said, "I am so sorry to hear it." I knew that was part of the emptiness I'd been feeling.

She also went on to say, "Kevin was telling everyone different stories. The real truth is his father used to beat him severely in order to bully him to be straight. His mother, a Catholic nurse, didn't intervene."

I began to understand that Kevin spent his entire life trying to get his father's approval. Then he killed himself after he learned that the approval was going to cost him far too much. It was a sad revelation. I always knew that Kevin's self-esteem was very fragile. It seemed to explain for me why Kevin got involved with spanking and violence in his search for sex. He probably felt that's all he deserved.

* * *

As Esther got even older, she had a stroke and needed to find an assisted-living place. She called me to tell me that her (evil) stepdaughters put her in a place in Minnetonka that was impossible for her son, Charles, to visit. He didn't drive and the buses didn't go there. She asked me to find her something better that suited her and Charles. I wasn't sure what assistance I could offer. I finally called her back with a senior ombudsman's telephone number and told her to ask them for help. I was driving to Southdale on Xerxes Avenue, and there, over the Crosstown Freeway, was a large banner that read "Assisted Living" with a phone number. I jotted it down, and later, I called Esther. She told me that she was moving into that very building in a couple of weeks. The senior help line gave her the lead, and she followed it.

Of course, that immediately changed our relationship. There were several weeks when I didn't see Esther. Then I tried to go to the assisted-living place and treat her there. It was awkward and difficult. Finally, I suggested that I could drive to her, pick her up, take her to the office, and then we could have lunch together before I dropped her off again. This became the established routine for some time. I made my Tuesdays, around the lunch hour, available for Esther.

* * *

I also continued to volunteer at Aliveness Project on Monday evenings. Sometimes I had more patients there in an hour and a half than in my office all week. I liked to have conversations with the guys and an occasional woman. Each one seemed to manage their disease in their own way. Not all of the HIV-positive people were gay. It was a curious subculture. Most of the members were secretive and didn't want to talk a lot about their condition. Many had employment difficulties, and most had side effects and discomfort from the medicines that they were on. By 2000, most of the multiple-pill regimens had given way to a few tablets per day. I saw the decline and death of many young talented men and women in the 80s and 90s. Some of them had become good friends.

The new century had better drugs and fewer deaths, but life for someone with the virus was not one of optimum health by any means. I encouraged the people I treated to have some humor, and I enjoyed allowing them to feel sexual and flirtatious. So many of the gay community who aren't infected seemed to have a callous attitude of "You should've known better" and "That's what happens when you are a bottom."

The reality is that HIV tends to spread through anal sex from a top to a bottom, but it isn't always the case. HIV is rarer in the lesbian community but not unheard of. Since the eighties, many gay men who were riding high with pride entered a deep depression that shadowed the culture from then on. I credit the lesbians for picking up the ball and advancing our path toward acceptance and equality. Many gay men were torn between trying to be sympathetic to infected friends and distancing themselves from the disease. By 2000, a rift existed between those who were infected and those that were clean. Those infected early were usually dead, and those uninfected felt everyone else should know better by now. I also wondered why I was seeing more young men and women at Aliveness after all the promotion of safe sex.

I understand how one sometimes has to build a wall to protect themselves from the attending emotions and discomfort of knowing someone with HIV. I, myself, stopped reading the obituaries and rarely went to funerals any more. But I also felt sympathy for those living with the virus and tried to understand and help those people. Maybe I had some survival guilt. In practice, I was asked quite often about the risks of one type of sex over another. In reality, it has to be fresh blood or body fluid directly from an infected person to the blood of an uninfected person. Even then, it has to be under nearly perfect circumstances. Why didn't I listen to myself?

It is easier to put a big wall up between clean and infected than to have to deal with uncertainties. That's what most people do. They treat AIDS as they once did leprosy. Once one has buried so many acquaintances, it's emotionally draining to dwell on the condition. For those of us that were coming out in the sixties and seventies, our new option was safe sex (nonspontaneous, barrier sex) or none at all. Many of my friends chose to have no sex or only masturbation. Jack-off clubs came into being in some parts of the country. It all seemed so far away from the free love and sex of the hippie days.

* * *

Art and I continued to go to St. Martin regularly. We actually went there more than once a year sometimes. Each time, as the plane approached the island, a sense of warmth and new adventure invaded my body. The aqua water was so beautiful, and the irregular landscape with all the hidden coves seemed spectacular. The plane glided over the water to land on the short runway that jutted out toward the sea. When the plane door opened, the warm moist tropical air slowly permeated the entire airplane.

I tried to trade my Breezy Point time-share for a back-to-back week with our St. Martin time-share. It worked once, when we stayed at The Towers for our first week. It was a rainy time of the year.

* * *

One memorable time we had was going to Happy Bay. We found the lovely cove. We were the only ones on the beach. There were palm trees for shade right near the sea. We sunned naked and frolicked in the clear, calm ocean water. To get to this beach, one has to climb a goat path up a steep hill and then down the other side. We found our way easily enough. After just an hour or so, dark clouds began to approach over the mountain. We just got into a temporary half-built shelter, when the clouds dumped pouring rain on us for over an hour. I've never seen so much water drop from the skies. It seemed unending. Art and I waited and looked for a break in the rain. Then we decided to accept the fact that we'd get drenched and started up the mountain. I was wearing flip-flops that slid in the muddy path and sometimes got sucked into the mud. Eventually I took them off and went barefoot. Descending the other side, the path had become a river of floodwater, and we laughed as we both soaked up the rain. We were covered with mud. Driving back, many of the roads were under water. We had to travel deliberately fast so that the car wouldn't become flooded. We'd been to St. Martin so many times by then that we knew where the roads were even when they were obscured by floodwater.

Later that week, we were on the sixth floor of our building, having a glass of wine and watching Dr. Phil, when the earth and our wine glasses shook. We knew from Palm Springs that it'd been an earthquake but didn't know that it was common for them to occur in St. Martin too.

The next year, when I tried to get a back-to-back trade, we didn't get one. We had already booked our plane tickets for a two-week stay. We ended up staying at a gay, clothing-optional resort, Delphina, which was run by two Germans. The buildings were new and the accommodations were adequate. The Germans didn't make very good hosts. We were charged for a glass of ice, and we had to pay extra for a ratty beach towel with a daily rental fee. There wasn't any ice machine on the premises. The hot tub wasn't heated and hadn't been cleaned for some time. The swimming pool was near a swamp, and there were always mosquitoes. It was clothing-optional, but the owners also gave a deal to parents and visitors of the nearby medical university. So I was out at the pool lying naked while a woman in her 70s was reading fifteen feet away, wearing a one-piece matronly swimsuit. Breakfast was dried bread and cheese and meats with a small assortment of fruits, unless one spoke German. Germans were offered hard-boiled eggs and sausage as well.

After one week there, we got to The View and practically begged to buy a second week. At our favorite beach, Cupecoy, Art and I were lying naked on the sand. A dark-colored young French guy put his blanket near Art. When I started a conversation with him, Art moved to the outside so that the Frenchman and I could hear each other better. His name was Etienne. He was twenty-one and was from Southern France, working here as a waiter. He was very attractive. He told me that he was half-Egyptian and half-Italian, but his family moved to France when he was very young. I was having fun practicing my French with him. After talking about a half hour, he said that he was going up to the top of the cliffs and hoped that I'd join him there for sex. Of course, I was flattered. He got up and left. I looked at Art.

Art asked me, "Where's the French man going?"

I answered, "He's going up the hill and wanted me to follow him to play."

Art asked me, "Are you going to go?"

I said, "I think it'd be a missed opportunity if I don't follow him."

Art replied, "Go ahead, but be safe."

So I did. I found him down a grassy path in a thicket of small trees. We both got naked and he swallowed my cock. I was going to do the same to him when I noticed that he had warts around the tip of his penis. I decided to just stroke him a little. He wanted me to enter him but I had no supplies, and I turned his mind away from that idea. When we both had orgasms, we went back down to the beach and jumped in the ocean to rinse off.

All in French, while in the water, I said to him, "I am fifty-two."

Etienne seemed shocked.

Then I added, "I was in France in 1970."

He said, "Wow, you could be my father!" He was twenty-one.

Back on our respective towels, I lay on my stomach to let the warm sun bake my ass. I gazed toward the young man and saw that there were now two more French guys near him. They were looking at my gluts. From behind my sunglasses, I noticed that erections were sprouting from both of the newcomers.

Etienne was close enough to me that I was able to hear him whisper to me in French, "David, you have a beautiful ass."

It was one compliment that I really needed and was happy to receive. The attentions of the other two reinforced the compliment.

* * *

Perhaps one reason Art and I enjoy St. Martin is that it's such a beautiful and sensual island. Our very first dinner on the island was at an outdoor table in a restaurant overlooking the sea. We had a cute server, and there were several adult couples looking longingly into each other's eyes. A photographer came around and snapped a photo of one couple. The man protested because he didn't want a copy of the photo ever to circulate to his wife, who wasn't present. Art and I joked about our waiter and wondered if when his shift ended, he might visit us in our studio. Our waiter must have overheard our conversation because he tripped nearby and nearly spilled the drinks he was porting.

One time, we were driving to the French side to go to a restaurant when an utterly stunning man in uniform got our attention. He was hitchhiking along the side of the road. While we rarely stop to pick up hitchhikers, we both agreed that we had to help out the man. The young man got into the backseat, and we soon learned that he was a pilot for the little commuter planes that ferried travelers to the other nearby islands. He was French and was on his way home to have dinner with his ... wife. Darn. But he knew the restaurant that we were headed to, and I had a good conversation with him in French. He was a stud.

There was the time that Art and I were at Cupecoy Beach, and a tall young French man began a conversation with us. His name was Xavier. His English lover had left him on the island an extra couple of weeks while he went back to work unexpectedly. Xavier was lonesome and joined up with us for a few days. We all were naked when we first met on the beach. We invited him back to our room and played. Later, we all went to dinner together.

Xavier kept asking me, "David, does Art earn enough money to make you happy?" He thought that I was Art's kept man.

I tried to explain, "Art and I are a couple, and we each make our own money."

But he didn't quite understand. He was a fun, playful, gentle man; and all of us seemed to have a good time. Later in the week, he abandoned us for a French gay couple, and we went our separate ways.

Another time, we were on a beach when we began a conversation with a cook, who worked on one of the many huge yachts that came into the harbor. It was very interesting and educational to hear from one who serviced the rich on their boats. These ships are multimillion dollar vessels with staffs of anywhere from five to twenty. He came back to our place for drinks, but neither Art nor I were interested in him sexually. I dropped him off after a few beers near the docks so he could go back to work.

St. Martin is romantic, unpredictable, sensual, and warm all at the same time. The food is almost always good; and before long, we learned how to have a great time, relax, and economize. Our time-share really became our home away from home. It was an escape for both of us that we desperately needed from the harsh Minnesota winters.

Chapter Thirty-One

2004

Every New Year, I tend to measure my life by what occurred in the past and where I want to go in the future. So by the New Year 2004, I was feeling reflective again. There were things that I was proud of and a few things that I knew I needed more work on. The backyard where we lived was a little oasis. We had our pond of water lilies and goldfish. There was also a pergola that I designed and built. We also had the hot tub. While we used the hot tub all winter, it wasn't used as frequently in winter as it was during the other seasons of the year.

My car was seven years old and had served me well. The first Monday of the New Year, I drove to Aliveness Project thinking things in my life were pretty good. It was a bitterly cold January night. The sun had already set by the time I parked my car on the busy street in front of the building. I walked in and immediately began to treat my regulars to my services. I was only working on the second person when there was a commotion that interrupted me.

Someone entered the room I was working in and announced, "A speeding car just crashed into your parked car."

The driver didn't stop but continued around the corner and took off. I went out into the frigid night and saw my car. The driver's door was smashed in, and most of the left side of the car was mangled. There was broken glass all over. I was in shock. Another volunteer had his car damaged as well. The police were called and made a courtesy visit. However, they told me that since it was a hit and run, there's very little they could do but to file a report for my insurance.

I'd only recently discontinued my collision insurance, thinking the car was old, and I wouldn't get much money back if I were in a collision.

The cold, the dark, and the depression left me in a state of mind, where I couldn't think clearly. I wasn't sure if I should have the car towed to a junkyard or to a body repair shop. A friend from the Project gave me a ride home, and I cried when I told Art that I no longer had a car.

I talked to my brother-in-law, who is a used car salesman, and he agreed to look at the car in the daylight and tell me if I should get it repaired or junk it. The next day, he called me after he scouted the damage and told me that it could be repaired. It might cost at least a couple thousand dollars to get it driving again. It'd probably cost as much to buy a different car that had so few miles on it. The good news was that the license plate from the car that hit me fell off upon impact and was lying under the debris of my disabled car. I went to Jeff and Paula's house and picked up the plate.

I called the police right away and was told to bring the plate into the station and hand it over to the man at the front desk. I did that and then waited to hear that it was received. When no one called me, I called the policeman who wrote up the report. He said that he had received it but had no other information. Art was able to find out who the owner of the license plate was and gave me that information. We were planning to go to St. Martin in a few weeks, and I thought I'd let the cops do their work without interference from me.

The very next week, our beloved dog Nikki Sioux died of old age. She had two litters of purebred puppies and was the sweetest and most well-behaved dog that I've ever owned. I began to feel as if 2004 was going to be a horrible year. When I told Esther about my losses, she was sympathetic and helped me to put my losses into perspective. Art let me use his old pickup truck because he'd recently bought a new small SUV. The winter was just beginning, but very soon, we were off to our island getaway for two weeks. As always, we had a good time in the balmy climate and the warm seas.

When we returned to Minnesota in February, I was still driving Art's old pickup, but my car was soon to be finished. I believe it was

going to cost close to $2,400. To save some money, I chose not to
get the new parts painted and not to fix the rear door that was badly
dented but functional. When it was done, the car resembled a police
squad car because it had a black front panel and a white door. The
rest of the car was the original toreador red. On my day off, I went
down to city hall to get a copy of the police report. I was planning on
taking the owner of the other vehicle to court or at least to get some
insurance money from the owner. I paid a small fee for the report. I
asked if there was another part of the report because I saw that the
officer hadn't written anything in the report about the license plate.
There weren't any other amendments. I realized that the police, who
didn't want to be bothered with more work, must've thrown away
the evidence so that they'd be finished with my case.

* * *

February was cold, and for diversions, Art and I sometimes rented
porn videos to enhance our romance. Art drove us to Panorama
Video on Lake Street, and I went in while Art parked his SUV. As
I entered the back room where the adult section was located, I saw
a man in his early twenties with his fly open. He was playing with
himself and wasn't alarmed that I noticed him. No one else was in
the room, so I moved closer to him. He showed me his penis that
was excited, and I knelt down and began to suck on him. Just as the
young man was having an orgasm, Art walked into the room and
was clearly distressed. It was a cataclysmic wake-up call for me.

It's only at that point that I realized how all my previous actions
impacted our relationship. I'd selfishly gone about trying to deny
my aging by taking dangerous risks that not only threatened my
health and life but also the health of Art and the stability of our
long-term relationship. It was a slap in Art's face and a slap to my
own. I was finally embarrassed by my behavior. From that point on,
I decided that I owed it to Art and to myself to try to stop taking
such dangerous risks, especially the risks of unsafe sex. But of course,
I was also deeply into denial, and my addictive behavior had already

been firmly implanted. It was going to take great effort to remodel my bad behaviors. By now, it'd become a true addiction.

* * *

I was determined to make positive changes, and I knew that it wouldn't always be easy. The first things were fairly easy. I didn't renew any of my memberships in the gay online Web sites. I could still access them but couldn't easily contact men directly. Many of the most provocative photos were now off-limits. I rechanneled my volunteer work to be more intense on healing and service instead of conversation. I stopped joking so much with the members at Aliveness Project about sexual activities. I looked at pictures of guys on the Internet but never took the initiative to engage anyone in computer conversations. And I refused to split my workday into pieces to accommodate sex.

Since the previous year, our governor, Jesse Ventura, lobbied and got domestic-partner health benefits included for state employees. That meant that I finally had decent health insurance again without much direct cost to me. Thank you, Jesse, who was in my class in junior high and high school. I had to change my driver's license to be registered at Art's address, but I'd been living there for years anyway. The drugs that I'd found for sale on the Internet in Canada were now again included in my state health plan.

In late February, I developed a cough and fever. I had some night sweats and felt weak, and sometimes I shook with chills. Since I had insurance now, I went to my doctor. He explained that I had a virus, and he couldn't do anything to help me. I asked him if I could at least get some medication for the severe cough that I had at night. He wrote a prescription for Vicodin, the same drug Dad took for pain when he was dying of prostate cancer.

The Vicodin helped me sleep more soundly, and after three or four weeks, I was much improved. I'd never been sick before like this and it scared me. I decided to go to The Red Door to have some tests for venereal disease. I was very relieved to find out that I was still HIV negative. I hadn't tested since Art and I first started seeing each other some fifteen years earlier.

A few years earlier, my diabetes became harder to control again, and I was put on Metformin along with my Prandin. It became so difficult to figure out what was working that I stopped my experiments with Mexican coyote melon; however, I continued to grow the plants.

* * *

One very unexpectedly pleasant diversion of the year was a trip to New Orleans. Art and I decided to go there in May. We found a gay B and B and booked a five-day trip. Our home ground was halfway between Bourbon Street and The Garden District. We had a wonderful time sampling all the different types of food. There was music everywhere, and we were even able to attend a big festival that was held in the park just in front of the big cathedral. We also went on a plantation tour, where we saw three different plantations. We had a mint julep at Twelve Oaks, where they were preparing for a wedding. We went to a cemetery in the Garden District and visited the Audubon Zoo, where a rhino calf was newly on display. Our B and B was an old mansion that had beautiful grounds and a swimming pool. The story was that the original owner used live alligators to guard the house. They couldn't be bribed by tainted meat the way dogs could. It was a good escape for me from everything that was going on. Fortunately, it was also before Katrina destroyed much of the city.

We were also staying within blocks of one of Emeril's restaurants. We enjoyed watching him on the Food Channel and decided to try his restaurant. It was very "shi-shi" and we felt underdressed. After I finally ordered, the server was gone for ten minutes before coming back to tell us he was out of my entree. The wine list didn't have any prices on it. I was intimidated enough that I ordered some wine that seemed familiar. My entrée was very average, and our bottle of wine cost $120. We were underwhelmed.

* * *

There were still long hours at work that were idle for me. Business didn't immediately pick up. I got involved in the politics of an election year. George Bush was running for a second term. John Kerry ran against him for the Democrats. Patients would come for treatments. I tried very hard not to let politics into the conversation. But once in a while, something was said, which I felt obligated to comment on or otherwise be put in a position of agreeing with something that I entirely disagreed with. Even though I had few Republican patients at the beginning of 2004, I had almost none by the time the election took place.

It was bad enough to lose patients to the ideology of politics. I was also losing them because of loss of employment, moving to other parts of the country, and attrition from death. I began to wonder what I should do in order to pay my bills. When I had too much downtime, I sometimes became depressed. I started to read murder mysteries to occupy my time. Many of the Web sites that I'd previously enjoyed going to upgraded, and it became more difficult to access any of them with dial-up service. To this day, I prefer dial-up so as not to get tempted back into computer sex.

* * *

Esther was one of my staunchest advocates. She rarely wavered from the schedule of every Tuesday around 11:00 AM. I would drive to her place at assisted living, where she'd be waiting. I helped her to get in the car, and we drove to my office for a treatment and lunch afterward. We did this rain or shine and even during the times when Esther needed to use a wheelchair. Though I don't think she read the newspaper and believe that she rarely watched television, she seemed to keep current with what was going on around her. One day when she came into the office after I had parked the car, she made a bold statement.

She said very emphatically, "Do you know that George Bush doesn't want gay people to get married! Isn't that the craziest thing you've ever heard?"

I said, "Esther, I have to agree with you."

Esther could lift me up just when I'd given up on most of the world. That summer, it seemed as if the rest of the world had given up on me. Business remained a trickle of what it used to be. I couldn't understand it. I was an excellent chiropractor and very fair and honest and truly concerned about my patients. My patients were very loyal, but many of them only came to see me once every two or three years. Sometimes, I wondered if I was too good and thought that maybe I should only half treat them as I suspected some practitioners did.

* * *

I filed the documents necessary to sue the individual whose car had damaged mine. I went to court that summer and confronted the woman who owned the car. She attempted to make a deal with me to charge her ex-boyfriend for the damage. He was already in jail for another issue. I told her that she was responsible since the car was registered to her. Of course, the judge agreed with me, and I won a settlement for four thousand dollars and court costs. Then, I found out that the woman didn't have insurance coverage and was a welfare mom with a couple of kids. She hadn't worked in years. I'm stuck with twenty years of trying to get blood from a turnip. It cost me a couple of hundred dollars for court fees, and I will most likely never get a penny from the woman responsible.

* * *

I decided that I'd have to remake my whole practice. I painted all the rooms with soothing colors and reupholstered my adjusting table. I moved the furniture around in new ways. I had the carpet cleaned. I tried to have a new attitude and a fresh outlook. Occasionally, I strayed and found a buddy on the Internet. Most of the time,

I came to rely on two particular guys. These two were unlike the others I'd met on the net. That is, I actually saw them more than the standard one time. They became real "fuck buddies" or "friends with benefits." Both of them enjoyed playing with me so much that they usually had more than one orgasm each time we were together. But of course, they had jobs and other obligations so we rarely met up more than once a month between the two of them. At my request, it was always spontaneous and only if our schedules could be easily coordinated.

One of my patients could see that I was having financial difficulties. She was a once-every-week massage and chiropractic patient. So she was already a big spender.

Then one day in July, she announced, "I've decided to move back to Colorado so that I can take care of my mother."

I jokingly put her on notice. I said, "You know that you're responsible to fill your void in my practice by referring a replacement."

Dane knew that she'd have to have her house painted in order to sell it. She called a few professional painters and got several bids. When she told me what the painter's wanted to charge, I asked her if I could make a deal with her.

I pleaded with her and asked, "Can I have the opportunity to paint the outside of your house for $20.00/hour or $500 less than the professionals, whichever is less?"

She agreed, and I began to split my time between her house in Roseville and my office in Minneapolis.

Several years earlier, Art and I had discontinued our landline in favor of cell phones. Quest was unable and unwilling to provide a static-free landline, and we didn't have any other options. I was able to forward my office calls to my cell phone and pretend that I was in my office, when I was actually up on a ladder scraping paint chips. Dane's next-door neighbor Azela asked me to paint her house as well and soon. I was racing to beat the onset of winter, which could start as early as mid-October in Minnesota. I was able to finish both houses before the weather turned too cold to paint outside. It was a big financial help and allowed me to pay most of my bills.

I occasionally managed to be bored enough that I again went online and looked at pictures of naked men. My new approach was never to be a first responder. The stranger would have to initiate everything. While I'd learned to be fairly successful in using the Web to navigate toward sexual reunions, in 2004, I began to have a high level of turndowns. Everyone seemed to only want someone who was forty or less and I was fifty-three but could easily pass for forty-three. I even experienced a time when someone dialogued with me about my picture on the Internet and insisted that I was lying about my age because they thought the picture couldn't be anyone who was forty-nine, which I'd put in the statistics. They thought the picture was someone more like forty-two. I deleted the picture of me when I was forty-eight and replaced it with a picture of when I was fifty-one and changed my age to fifty. Even then, I wasn't given much attention, which was actually okay by me.

The other requisite was that a person should be DDF (drug and disease free). As far as I knew, I was DDF; but I think sometimes, when I appeared in front of a stranger, my diabetic stomach, which seemed to get bigger with age, belied my age and colored a first impression negatively. I also wondered how sure everyone was about their own disease status. Even having a negative HIV test doesn't reflect the true health status of the previous six months. With the added scrutiny of strangers, I began to respond even less to new adventures.

Home life was actually improving because I didn't have as much to try to hide, and Art and I seemed to have better times. We used our hot tub more often, and Art seemed to use the home computer less when we were both home. We were down to a single dog, Kaiser, who'd finally come into his own after Nikki died. He became even more loyal and brave. In November of 2004, I began to notice that when Kaiser jumped off the bed or off the love seat, he'd yelp a little. He was only about ten years old, and I thought he was far too young and active to have arthritis.

In the meantime, Bush stole the election from Kerry by bringing up the specter of gay marriage so that the right-wingers in Ohio put Bush over the top. Never mind that Florida, which was governed by

Bush's brother, had numerous voting irregularities that gave Bush that state as well. Kerry never got a warm welcome from the entire Democratic Party. I'm still convinced that with Bush Jr., the United States didn't get free and fair elections.

And as I was thinking that things couldn't get much worse, a week before Thanksgiving, Kaiser took a turn for the worse. The week before Thanksgiving, he stayed in his bed most of the time. By the weekend, with both Art and myself home, he perked up a little. When I finally got him to socialize, I petted his head and discovered a golf-ball-sized lump on the side. I felt terrible, but I was sure that he had a brain tumor, and that's why he whimpered when jumping down from furniture. Art and I discussed the situation. I made an appointment with the vet and decided that I might have to put him down.

I took Kaiser in on my day off. The vet took some blood samples and felt the lump but was unsure of a diagnosis. I heard the results of the lab tests a few minutes later. Those findings were still inconclusive. The vet encouraged me to spend more money with CAT scans and surgery, if necessary. I told the vet that I was sure of what this was and that I'd nurse him as best I could until he needed last rites. Then I'd bring him back and say good-bye.

It was so sad. Art and I both realized that we had very few photos of Kaiser, so we tried to take a bunch of last-minute pictures. I'd read about the wonders of turmeric in causing tumor cells to die while not harming good cells. I started sprinkling turmeric on Kaiser's food. For about a week, I was greatly encouraged when I noticed the lump on his head growing smaller. Kaiser's energy and disposition also seemed to be improving. But by the end of the second week, while the lump had disappeared, Kaiser began to show more neurological impact. His vision deteriorated, and his hearing was almost totally gone. Around Christmas, we decided that we'd have to bring him in to the vet for euthanasia. The only time that we could all go together was New Year's Eve. I didn't want to have the memory of his death every New Year, so I told Art that I'd take him in myself a few days before the New Year.

I took him in, and I believe he was aware of exactly what was happening. He walked in very deliberately, even though he used to hate going to the vet's office. His head was in a forced extension, probably because of the internal pain. I was with him the last few moments alone and petted him and cried. I told him what a wonderful dog he'd been and how brave he was. It was over in very few minutes. The vet helped me wrap him in a blanket. I carried him to the car and noticed how heavy he seemed in death. I guess that's why they refer to it as deadweight.

Both dogs had died that year, each of them in the winter. We put them each in our downstairs freezer alone until we could bury them when the ground thawed out. We buried Nikki in April up at our lake property and Kaiser, the following April, in the backyard. By the end of that year, I lost the two dogs, I lost a big part of my car, I almost lost my business, Kerry lost the election, and I didn't know it at the time, but I'd lost my foundation for good health.

* * *

Another source of sadness for me was Esther. While she was in assisted living, I picked her up and took her to treatment and lunch. I watched her as she began to slowly fail right before my eyes. At first, it was little things. She'd sometimes drop her spoon on the floor. But gradually, she spilled the soup from her spoon onto the front of her dress. Sometimes, she was unable to grip her sandwich, and the contents would fall on her clothes. I wanted to put a bib on her, but I knew that she, too, was aware of her gradually increasing problems with dexterity. Then once, I came to pick her up and she wasn't ready. I went in and found her still in her nightclothes. She was in a lot of pain from arthritis. I worked with her as best I could right there in her room. Management told me that if she didn't improve significantly, they would have to move her to a nursing home. And then a few weeks later, she got surprisingly better, and they gave her a reprieve.

Chapter Thirty-Two

The Magic Ring

By New Year 2005, I had another year to reflect on. I hadn't heard from Esther for a couple of months. It seemed odd, but I missed her and her impartial company. Not far into the New Year, I got a call from Charles, Esther's son. He asked me if I'd start seeing his mother again on a regular basis. I agreed to start again, but when I called at her old assisted-living place, I was told she was no longer there. I wasn't given any more information because I was not family. I called Charles again, and he told me his mother was now at a nursing home. He said she was on the top floor of the building on Xerxes, Edina Care Center. He said that I should punch a keypad with a code to gain entrance to her wing. And he gave me the code.

He was correct. Esther was on the third floor. Before entering from the parking lot, which never had enough spaces, I had to disable the alarm. I walked in. In front of me was a large desk with a nursing station. No one was around, and I finally found someone who seemed to work there and asked them where I might find Esther. They told me I had to go through another set of doors, and her room would be near the beginning of the hallway after that. I went through the doors, and sure enough, I saw Esther's name on the second door on my left. Esther had a roommate. Esther's eyes lit up as she saw me. She was in bed and had just come back from eating lunch.

Esther had another stroke a few months earlier, and because she was restless, she was put in the locked ward with those who had moderate to severe mental disabilities. She didn't seem very disabled to me.

She beamed as she said, "Charles told me you were coming."

We chatted and got caught up on what was going on in the last few months. Although Esther wasn't that happy with her current situation, she seemed resigned to acceptance. The food was okay and she was warm. Her roommate was in far worse condition than she. In fact, Esther had a different roommate almost every month because they kept dying. I'd gotten a new portable Alpha Stim machine that was supposed to stimulate positive brain waves to reduce pain and increase energy. I used it on Esther, set it for an hour, and started to give her a bed massage. She was beyond the point of manually adjusting her bones.

Esther was a captive audience. For an hour, we talked about anything that would keep her interested. Esther told me I was her walking newspaper. She showed me a cheap ring that Charles gave her and talked about it as if it were quite valuable. She noticed my ruby ring and admired it. Charles came to visit his mother almost every day. When he didn't come, he called her on the telephone. Esther still had her special phone that allowed her to turn up the volume. She didn't have much of a view from her room and could only see the rooftop of the next building. It was a change for her and for me. It seemed somewhat depressing, but her spirits didn't seem low.

As I was leaving, I asked, as I always did, "Do you want me to come again next week?"

She replied, "Yes, I would like that very much. Take the check from the top drawer that Charles wrote for you."

I charged Esther a small fee because she didn't want charity, but it wasn't very much, considering my travel time and a full hour of bodywork.

As I was leaving, I realized that I was in a locked ward, and the doors, which led to the exit, were closed and painted in trompe l'oeil to look like a tall cupboard. I had a slight panic and fantasized that someone would come along and say to me, "Now, David, you know that you can't leave here. This is your home now." I soon found a nurse who told me the secret code and where the code pad was located. I wondered if the code was always the same or if they would change it someday without telling me.

Esther told me almost a year earlier that she'd soon outlive all of her savings and retirement money. Just before the market crashed, her advisor pulled her money out of her Putnam funds and put it in a savings account. Now it was all gone. Yet she wanted to see me every week, and I was happy to visit her.

After 9/11, Esther remarked, "People are so obsessed with flying flags. Suddenly everyone is a patriot. If you don't jump on the bandwagon, you're suspected of being a terrorist."

I loved the way she expressed herself. Esther had managed to live into her nineties and still was bold enough and unafraid to voice her opinions and concerns. I began to look at her as a positive role model for aging gracefully. She still had a youthful spirit, and her self-esteem was so strong.

* * *

When one grows up to discover that they're gay, there are very few role models to look to. Especially in the 1960s, coming out was a rogue thing. The immediate observation is that there's a community of other gays and lesbians. However, that encompasses people with all sorts of deviations from normal. It sometimes feels like you've joined a group that you never really wanted to associate with. Without the possibility of marriage and social recognition, romance has to be subtle and discreet. Heterosexual couples can hold hands, kiss, and embrace. Onlookers usually are reminded of when they, too, were in love. When two men do the same thing, they can be harassed, ridiculed, and sometimes even arrested. With a de facto prohibition of overt sexual posturing, there's little overt role modeling taking place. When it comes to aging, there's almost an unrealistic abhorrence for being an old queer among gay people.

I was having a difficult time going from being a boy toy to becoming a respectable middle-aged faggot. Even searching the ads on the Internet is very age biased. The ads usually want someone less than age forty, tops. After that, you're supposed to be dead or locked into a long-term relationship. Certainly, you're not to be looking for sex at ages over fifty. I've always wondered if twenty-eight-year-olds ever believe they're going to get to age fifty and beyond. But for me, I try to look at age as only a number. The sad thing is that since AIDS, there are very few of my contemporaries still alive. Most of them are not very active in sexual terms. Many are retired and have moved to warmer climates.

* * *

Maybe that's why I love going to St. Martin so much. It's warm there. Shortly after reuniting with Esther, Art and I left for our now two-week trip to the Caribbean. It was the first time that we didn't have dogs to worry about back home. We settled into our time-share fast, and after our major grocery store adventure, we were ready for the beach. Cupecoy Beach was in its glory. There was a lot of sand, and the ocean was warm and beautiful. About the third day, we arrived at the beach and noticed the waves were large, and the surf was intimidating. There were a few people out swimming.

I was anxious to go into the water, and I watched to see how others made it in and out with all the whitecaps. In a little while, the sea seemed a bit calmer. I told Art I was going in. He warned me to be careful. I was only in the water a short time and thought to myself that I should consider getting back out as soon as the next bunch of waves passed. Then I committed a cardinal sin by turning my back to the sea. A huge high roller broke over my head and started to spin me in circles. I was struggling. I had an out-of-body experience as I saw myself thrashing around violently. As I watched myself, I saw and felt my ruby ring get pulled off my finger and tumble in wide loops downward toward the bottom of the sea. I tried to hold my breath as long as I could and tried to ride the wave into shore. I realized I'd lost my ring, and I said to myself, somewhat foolishly, "I hope it lands somewhere that I can find it again." I washed up on the shore, glad to be alive, but without my ring.

I was shaken. I went to where Art laid on the sand.

I almost cried as I blurted out to Art, "My ring got sucked off my finger." I showed him my empty ring finger.

I went to the water's edge and wondered if a ring could possibly ever roll to shore someday. Cupecoy is notorious as a beach of shifting sand. I knew that if my ring fell into the sand, it was surely lost forever. I wondered if the universe was telling me that with the loss of my relationship ring, my relationship with Art was also coming to an end. After all that I'd endured last year, I started thinking that everything might just keep getting worse in spite of the New Year. Several times before we left the beach, I went to the shoreline and scanned the tide. I even talked to a few other people and asked them to be on the lookout for a ruby ring. Then we went home.

The next couple days, we searched almost all the fine-jewelry stores in St. Martin to try to find an identical replacement ring. No one seemed to be selling men's ruby rings anymore. Two evenings later, on the way to dinner, we stopped by a store that sold a mishmash of things including fine jewelry. An Indian man was happy to show us his rings and admitted that he didn't have any ruby rings. He showed us a similar ring that was made up of blue diamonds. He said that blue diamonds were all the rage now. The ring was attractive and after bargaining back and forth, I decided to buy it.

At that point, Art stepped up and said, "I'll buy it for you."

When Art volunteered, I had a hopeful thought that maybe our relationship wasn't over. The Indian kept the ring for sizing.

The next morning, there was a presentation at the time-share. One of the sisters who run our resort, Martina, talked to us about her massage and energy work. She talked about positive energy. I asked Martina what she thought about the possibility of finding a ring lost in the ocean. When she found out it was lost at Cupecoy, she said it might never be found, and if it was to be found, I'd probably need to hire scuba divers to sift through the sand underwater.

I was determined to find it myself. I looked out at the sea and noticed that it seemed very calm at the moment.

I said to Art, "I want to go to Cupecoy and snorkel just to see if there's any chance of finding my ring."

He agreed and said, "Let's go." But I could tell he didn't want to encourage me to fail.

I decided to think very hard about exactly what I'd see if I looked down on my ring from above. I burned the image into my brain as a template and knew that I had to match that image with a vision from my eyes.

We got to the beach. The ocean was calmer than I'd ever seen it before. There was a couple on the beach from a cruise ship.

They saw me carrying my snorkel gear and asked, "Is snorkeling good here?"

I said, "It's usually pretty choppy here, but I'm on a search and rescue mission to find my ring." I explained to them that I lost it three days earlier.

Their only response was, "Good luck."

I was only in the water a few minutes, looking at the sea bottom when, all of a sudden, I saw the circle of my ring lying on a rock ledge. It was a match to the template in my brain. I couldn't believe it. I quickly dove down and was able to pick up the ring, which was under eight feet of water. I rushed to the shore and ran up to Art and showed him the ring.

The couple couldn't believe it either and said, "You should go to the casinos right now."

Then I had the thought that maybe the universe was saying to me, "Once you realize that you can get along without the ring, the ring will come back."

On our way back, we ran into Martina, and I showed her the ring. I showed several people the ring at the resort, and I still like to tell the story every time my ring is admired. To this day, I think if I hadn't found my ring, I would go to Cupecoy and always wonder if it's still in the sea or if someone else had found it. Art still wonders if it was all a ploy to get another new ring.

The rest of our trip was a celebration of new hope and a determination that I would try harder in our relationship. When we got back, I told Esther about the ring. She was surprised and very happy that I found my ring again. Many times afterward when I visited, she asked to see my ruby ring again.

Chapter Thirty-Three

Bush's Second Term

Once Bush was sworn in for a second term, I decided that I wasn't going to buy into his stupid "everything is rosy" scenario. Now we had an enemy, be it Al-Qaeda or the Taliban or the terrorists. The stock market wasn't the growing machine of the '90s. I made a decision to pull out a large part of my investment stocks and look to real estate for an opportunity to make money. I put a chunk of money into a savings account and found a realtor who was also a patient of mine.

In February, we started looking for a small house that I could own and rent out as my new investment. First, I looked on the west and south side of Minneapolis, which seemed to have the most desirable addresses. I had a limited amount of money I could put down, and after several run-down houses in the "good" neighborhoods, I began to be more open to other areas. A few times, I looked at houses in the near north side, but I felt uncomfortable there. I decided that my choice of houses had to be made from a perspective of "would I live there?"

I'd learned to use my computer for MLS Web sites, where I could keep track of several different houses at a time. In April, I found a house in Camden, a neighborhood on the northwest edge of Minneapolis. I drove by it; I had my realtor look into it for me. Eventually, we bid on the house and the bid was accepted. It was a home of an old woman, who'd recently died but had lived in the house since 1954. It was a small two-bedroom house with an extra wide lot, which was an asset.

I was somewhat upset because while I was buying a house, I was actually buying an investment house. Because I wasn't going to be living there, I was required to put 20 percent down. The appraisal and closing costs all seemed to double as everyone wanted to get their hands on my investment dollars. Once I succeeded in buying the house, I was required to fix everything on the "Truth in Housing" list, and of course, I had to pull permits and could only hire a licensed professional to do any work. I bought the house because I was capable of doing most of my own repairs and improvements, only to discover that I wasn't allowed to do that.

My very first order of business was to add new gas valves at the stove and furnace. I had a plumber come out who charged one hundred dollars just to give me an estimate. If I didn't like the estimate, I paid one hundred dollars, and he left; otherwise, the cost of the estimate would be reduced from the total bill. I wanted the work done, so I agreed to the estimate of $2,200. I added to the job by asking him to run a gas line from the supply to where I was going to put a gas dryer. I could've done all the work myself for about one hundred dollars. Then I had to have his work inspected. So a few days later, the plumbing inspector came and looked at the stove valve and dryer gas setup and approved it. I asked her about the new furnace valve inspection, and she told me that it had to be inspected by the heating inspector. What a racket! It was an early taste of why it doesn't pay to own rental property in Minneapolis.

I was able to find a good tenant and soon was getting some income from my property. My first tenant was a young woman, who signed a lease with her girlfriend. At the last minute, she replaced her friend on the lease with her own brother. Then those two shared the house.

* * *

After Art and I got back from St. Martin, our house seemed empty. There was no pitter-patter on the floor and no watchdog alarm. The tension between us escalated without having any outside circuit breakers. About the same time I was looking for houses, we discussed the possibilities of getting another dog. We watched the Westminster Dog Show, and I wrote down some possibilities for future dogs. I didn't want to have Westies anymore. After Nikki and Kaiser, I wanted to try another breed. I checked out several breeds, but everyone had advantages and disadvantages. Finally, I started to focus on cairn terriers. Cairns were an older breed, one that Westies were bred from.

I began to peruse the weekend want ads. Cairns were listed starting from around $200 up to $400. I didn't need to have a Westminster Champion, so when I saw a male dog listed for two hundred dollars, I showed the ad to Art. He agreed that I should call, and soon, that Sunday, we were on our way to Owatonna to look at puppies. We pulled into a farm that had three large barns. There were two puppies and two adult Cairns outside in a makeshift pen. An older man came out of the main house and greeted us. He ran quite the operation. He raised Cairns, Chihuahuas, Silkies, Yorkies, Westies, and pugs. Art and I looked at each other as we pulled into the long drive leading to the house and mumbled "puppy mill." The puppies were cute. We made our choice, Art paid, and we left.

On the way home, I asked Art, "Do you think that was really the mother? She didn't have any remnants of enlarged nursing breasts."

I figured that at least we'd rescued one puppy and that he'd have a good home.

I'd forgotten what it was like to have a young puppy in the house. Besides potty training, there was the teething and chewing and the discipline and training to a leash. There were vet's appointments and bills. And as we soon discovered, Teddy, our cairn, was a master escape artist. He was only four pounds when we got him but grew a little every day. It took him less than a week to learn how to navigate the back steps. We have a wooden privacy fence surrounding the backyard. On the inside of the fence, we had hostas planted. As terriers do, Teddy learned that he could use the cover of the big hostas to dig his way under the fence. We soon learned that he couldn't be in the backyard without constant supervision. It took him less than five minutes to dig an exit hole and disappear.

Sometimes the neighbor next door who owned Ella, a pit bull, would ring the front door bell, carrying Teddy in her arms. Teddy was in love with Ella.

The summer of 2006, Teddy orchestrated the great escape. He managed to dig four holes under the fence under the cover of the hostas. Then in mid-June, I let him out while I was home from work during lunch. He escaped, and when I went to call him, there was no response. I opened the gate and looked down the alley to see if I could spot him. I finally saw him, and he came to me when I called him. Back inside the gate, I returned to the house, and in minutes, I heard Teddy barking several houses north of ours. Again, I found him and put him inside the fence. Then I went all along the fence and discovered there were three more holes that I needed to plug with rocks. He'd been planning all spring for this great escape.

Teddy trained us to push chairs all the way under the tables, or otherwise, he'd jump up on the chairs and onto the table. I left the house once with a full stick of butter on a plate on the table but left a chair out. He managed to get up on the table and eat the entire stick of butter. Then he regurgitated all of it on the carpet below.

When I told Esther about the butter incident, she laughed out loud. Several visits later, she was still asking me if the dog had eaten any more butter. I had a new digital camera and once in a while, I'd print up a full-page picture of the yard or of Teddy. I gave them to Esther. She put the pictures in places of honor and kept them handy to look at between visits.

Shortly after we got Teddy, I took off my ruby ring and left it on the table next to my chair where I watch TV. When I went to look for it the next morning, it was gone. I searched all over the house but to no avail. I wondered if maybe the dog had eaten it, so I followed him everywhere, thinking it may drop out of his other end. After about two weeks, I picked up all of his droppings from the yard and rented a metal detector. I ran the detector over the bag of droppings and all around the yard. No luck. I tried it inside the house, but too many metallic interferences made the detector worthless. I figured that he might've flung it at a wall like he sometimes does with his other toys. I searched the basement. Nine months later, when I was getting the snorkeling fins from under the bed, I discovered Teddy's stash of chewed underwear, shredded socks, and my ruby ring under the bed. It was at the top, middle part of the bed, almost unreachable from either side.

By the end of 2005, *Brokeback Mountain* was a big movie hit and was nominated for an Academy Award for best picture in 2006. Art and I went to a movie theatre to watch it. We rarely went to the movies. That movie had a big impact on me. I cried through most of the last thirty minutes, and when we emerged from the theatre, I was still sobbing. The movie made me really think about my relationship with Art and how, at any moment, it could all end tragically. I really wanted to secure our relationship and strengthen our bond. I knew that I had to totally stop playing Russian roulette with strangers and having unprotected sex and also that I had to account for everything I'd done previously. I decided that I'd let some time pass and then go to the Red Door and get tested for sexually transmitted diseases. Once cleared, I wanted to recommit with Art and be monogamous.

Chapter Thirty-Four

Committing a Fatal Error

January 2006 was another two weeks in St. Martin. Back in December 2005, when we went to Breezy Point for a few days, we tried a home dog-sitting service for Teddy, who was only eight months old. This was a woman who'd been a patient. She regularly took dogs into her home for boarding. When I went to pick him up, I asked how things went.

The woman started to cry and said, "It was horrible."

I asked, "Can I bring him again sometime?"

She said, "Please take the dog. I never want to see him again."

I felt bad for the woman. Then I realized that she'd discarded all of Teddy's favorite toys that we brought for him to play with. He loved to take the empty plastic Smirnoff bottle and throw it into the wall and bounce it around. Apparently she was much more comfortable with old tiny toy-poodle lapdogs than with a young dramatic independent terrier. For our annual St. Martin trip, I hunted around and found a good kennel. We took him to that kennel. For two weeks, he was there. When we came to pick him up, the staff raved about him. Teddy didn't want to leave.

* * *

This time, St. Martin was somewhat subdued. I found my buried stash of marijuana, but I only smoked a little bit. We had some good meals out, and I cooked a few good meals in. We went to Cupecoy often and Orient Beach more than usual. Our trips were getting more relaxing with less new adventures. When we got home, I was determined to go and get tested, and I was anxious to start a more committed life with Art.

So on a Thursday, I made my way to the Red Door. It was the free STD testing site in Hennepin County. I signed in under a fake name and address. At first, I thought I'd only get tested for the normal STDs like syphilis and chlamydia. I hadn't had any symptoms that pointed to my immune system. But I figured while I was there, I might as well test for HIV.

The nurse that I was assigned to was the same one whom I'd seen in 2004. She reminded me of one of my patients. She was very efficient and not at all judgmental.

She asked, "Why are you here today?"

I answered, "I really want to clean up my act. I've been having sex with guys that I meet on the computer."

Then she asked me, "Do you use protection every time?"

When I answered, "No, not always."

She lightly scolded me for not always using protection. I tried to defend myself by letting her know that latex seemed to irritate my sensitive skin. She took some samples and then left me in the room alone.

For what seemed to be a really long time, I waited. After several minutes, I began to hear disruptions in the hallway, and I was sure that I heard several people scurrying about. I heard a call go out for a social worker over the intercom. My nurse came back into the room. The look that she gave me seemed foreboding.

In a sad voice, she said, "Well, your test in 2004 was negative. But I'm sad to tell you that today your HIV test came out positive."

I was devastated. I started to cry. I was in shock. I thought that I'd made my life's fatal error. I wouldn't have to consider longevity anymore. I worried that Art might be infected, all because of my behavior. The sky was falling, and my part as the healthy chiropractor and role model was yanked out from under me. A social worker came in and put his hand on my own. He asked me if I was okay. I just cried. He was concerned about what I was going to do next. I told him I was going to take my dog to the dog park and walk around. I was worried that when I told Art, that Art would want to leave me. I also wasn't sure how I could go on without health insurance and with such a low income.

The new Republican governor of Minnesota, Pawlenty, made it his first priority to take away health insurance benefits from same-sex partners of state employees. That left me (and eighty-eight others) without health insurance. I couldn't afford the cost of continuing insurance under the Cobra option.

The social worker gave me some pamphlets with answers to questions and resources. He assured me that there were programs out there to help me. There was an outside chance that the test I took was a false positive, and they'd be sure in another week. I saw my entire career and life vanish under an insurmountable stack of health bills. The only thing that I got some comfort in was the notion that I was no different today than I was yesterday. I was also given a confusing lecture about HIV transmission. On the one hand, I was told that HIV could only be spread by blood and body fluids mixing directly into another's blood and body fluids. This I understood. But then, I was told not to share drinking glasses, toothbrushes, or eating utensils. This seemed to be at odds with the earlier information.

I went home and got Teddy. He's always anxious to visit his favorite dog park. While it was still winter, that day there was a hint of thawing. When I took off the leash, Teddy ran ahead of me as I followed behind. I felt as if I had a big red light on my forehead that people could read, flashing the word "POSITIVE." I turned my head away from strangers. I was more aloof with people than ever before. Of course, Teddy acted as though nothing had changed. I was preoccupied with trying to figure out a way to tell Art. It seemed like the worst message I could ever give him. I went back to work, feeling as if my whole future was spinning out of control.

That night, I got home late. Art was already home. I walked in, and I couldn't help, it but I immediately started to cry.

Art came over and kissed me and asked, "What's wrong?"

I confided to him, "I got an HIV test today, and I tested positive." I tried to add, "I am so sorry," but I choked on my words.

Art kept saying, "Everything's going to be okay. Calm down. We can get through this."

I sat down in a daze.

After a few minutes, Art asked, "Why did you test?"

I just said, "I wanted to know." I could hardly speak.

Then the reality struck Art, and he said, "What about our monogamous relationship?"

I knew he had suspicions sometimes in the past, but I figured he probably didn't want to acknowledge that I'd been unfaithful.

All I could say was, "I really fucked up and I'm so sorry. I really hope that you aren't positive because of me."

I felt so hollow. I told him again and again how sorry I was. I only wished that I could somehow change my outcome, but I couldn't. I had no idea how I was going to deal with life, sickness, and lack of insurance. I wondered if I'd even be allowed to practice chiropractic. I also wondered what I was going to say or not say to patients. I kept saying to myself that I was the same person as I was a week ago.

I'd always prided myself with being healthy and young looking and able to defeat illness naturally. I agonized about the many friends I had lost to AIDS and remembered how sick they became and how fast they aged before my eyes. Often, it was a hideous and painful death.

I heard my father saying, "Until you have a condition yourself, you can't really understand what your patient goes through."

I'd witnessed firsthand the misery that HIV could bring to otherwise healthy, vibrant young men and women. Yes, the drugs were better than they were in the beginning. But care was expensive, and unless I became disabled, I'd have to figure out how to pay huge amounts of my income to stay healthy.

I went back to the Red Door a week later. I still had some hope that the test was a false positive. It wasn't false. I wasn't sure what my next step should be. I didn't feel any symptoms yet. I decided that I'd keep my eyes and ears open to find out what my options were going to be. I think they did some blood tests at the Red Door, like viral load and T-cell counts, but it was all a blur at that time.

I continued to volunteer at Aliveness Project, and I began to ask more questions from the more frequent members. Many of my closer friends there considered their infection a chronic health problem. But almost all of them had insurance. Some were on disability, some on early retirement, some on Medicare. It seemed to be time-consuming work to stay ahead of the HIV virus. Many of the members spent most of their day dealing with HIV. There were doctor appointments, gym memberships, and drugs to combat the side effects of the main HIV drugs. I'd gone from being a service provider to becoming a member of the club. I was beginning to understand why most of the members only wanted to be known by their first names.

* * *

While I felt as though I knew something about the stigma of AIDS in the twenty-first century, it was a rude awakening to suddenly be the one who was stigmatized. Most people were afraid and insecure. Many people were afraid of terrorists. People were afraid that they were going to lose their jobs. People were afraid that they wouldn't be able to buy adequate food and clothes for themselves and their families or even hang on to their homes. Insecurity was institutionalized by the Bush administration and the actions of 9/11.

Some people were also afraid that there was an infectious disease in gay people and drug addicts that could cause death. The educated knew that it's not easily transmissible. But there remained a lot of uncertainty and fear about transmission. People would rather avoid knowing an actual person who carried the disease. It's very close to being the leprosy of the new age. I understand all that, but now I was on the other side of it.

I began to be depressed and had sleepless nights, where I was consumed with self-loathing. The only bright spot in my fate was the revelation that Art tested negative when he went to the Red Door. I became preoccupied with worry. I worried about becoming so sick that I'd be unable to make a living. I was worried that

I'd progressively get many horrible, painful, and hard-to-deal-with complications. I worried about ageing even faster. I was always so open and up front with my patients, and now there was a dark barrier between them and myself.

I knew that depression and anxiety would only accelerate disease. I tried to be as upbeat as possible, but it was very hard. I expected some rejection and loss of patients if the knowledge that I was HIV positive was broadcast. I learned from those who went before me that anonymity and silence was often better than rejection. In some ways, the situation seemed similar to when I was coming out as a gay man. Sometimes silence was better than confrontation.

I decided that I'd try telling just a few close friends about my new status. One woman was a massage client whom I'd been seeing for six years every two weeks. I was giving the massage, and I waited toward the end of the session.

When I felt the timing was right, I said to her, "I decided to get myself tested for HIV."

She asked me, "What were your results?"

I answered honestly, "I tested positive."

I could feel her body get rigid immediately, and the rest of the massage went on in silence.

When she emerged from the massage room, she looked at me and said, "Well, David, I am sorry to say this, but I can no longer come here anymore for massage. I'm a germaphobe, and I'll never be able to relax again while you're touching me."

It was almost as if she were my lover, and she felt that I'd betrayed her. I told her that my actual lover, Art, had tested negative even a few years after I'd been positive. And we always had unprotected sex.

She said to me, "I'll e-mail you and keep in touch. Maybe we could have coffee together sometime."

It was a while before I dared to talk to anyone else about my status.

Of course, my mind kept grinding, trying to figure out when I was infected and who most likely infected me. Art wanted to know because he wanted to punish the guy. I knew it was either in late

2003 or early 2004. I knew that my "cold" back then was probably my body's reaction to the initial exposure. I'd tested negative in 2004, but the virus can take up to six months to become detectable. I soon realized that it'd be virtually impossible to come up with the one guy that could've transferred his virus to me. It's my own fault for allowing unsafe sex to occur in the first place. It wouldn't do anyone any good to find a name for the perpetrator. I finally had to let it go and accept my new plight.

I felt an obligation to inform those that I'd had sex with. Most of them were from years before and would remain anonymous. One guy I knew first as a patient. Years later, he moved to Texas, and we actually became personal friends. For a few years, he'd been calling me long distance every week to chat about his and my sexual encounters. He loved to hear about guys that I met online, and I'd tell him most of the things that happened from those encounters. When he called after I found out my status, I told him that my test for HIV came out positive. He was at first incredulous and then abruptly hung the phone up. I've never heard from him again.

Of course, my days of meeting anyone online or otherwise were over. No one wanted to play around with anyone who knew they were diseased. I didn't want to put anyone at risk either. It was all a very long cold shower. Even my two buddies needed distance from me. One of the guys later contacted me to see how I was doing. The other avoided me like the plague. I continued to feel very much alone. My own insecurities took over, and when I'd get a twitch or a pimple or a discoloration anywhere, I believed that my immune system was collapsing, and I was spiraling toward an early death.

I tried to keep a positive outlook but was haunted by visions of my friends who went before me and died tragic and horrible deaths. Even Liberace and Rock Hudson, with all their money, couldn't beat HIV. There was hope in Magic Johnson and many of the guys that I still treated at Aliveness Project. But honestly, the majority of the survivors looked as if they've been fighting an arduous battle. Many didn't seem as if they were really all that healthy. I worried that I'd begin to get the deep facial creases and the fatty deposits on my neck and back, which were side effects of some of the prevailing treatments. I knew some guys who went to Mexico to get injections on some of their facial creases. I was determined to come up with a plan for myself, where I could live a healthy long life in spite of the virus. Or maybe there'd be a cure found soon.

* * *

I continued to see Esther. I wondered if I'd be allowed into a nursing home if my condition were revealed. I was the same person that I'd always been in Esther's eyes. My weekly meetings with her gave me some consistency in my otherwise chaotic life. Once, I got to Esther's bed, and a head nurse and a social worker were already there.

The nurse said to me, "You can't see Esther any more without a doctor's order."

I responded, "I am a doctor."

She countered, "You can only see Esther with a written order signed by Esther's nursing-home doctor."

I bristled and looked directly at the nurse and said, "I guess you'll have to get busy and write up an order then because I intend to see Esther as long as Esther wants to me to see her."

I wondered if it had anything to do with the HIV virus. Maybe somehow it showed on me.

After they left, Esther asked, "What's all the fuss about?"

I summarized the situation for her and said, "Esther, I'll be here for you as long as you want me to be here."

Chapter Thirty-Five

Charting My Course

There seemed to be no hurry to get HIV treatment. My initial blood work showed that I'd probably been infected two years earlier. My T-cells were almost 400, and my viral load was about 36,000. Since viral load can get to be over two million, no one seemed concerned with my low levels. I had to start learning the vocabulary.

The two most important markers seem to be T-cell count and viral load. Normal T-cell count is 620 and higher. Normal viral load for an HIV person should ideally be undetectable, which is to say less than 50 viral particles in a small amount of blood sample. There are also several other blood profiles that are looked at, including liver and kidney function, other blood tests, and blood counts of other types of blood cells. Fortunately from my studies in chiropractic, I was at least somewhat familiar with most of the blood tests.

I decided that I wasn't going to share my HIV status and progress with Esther. I didn't want Esther to have to worry about me. In 2005, I decided not to tell her about Katrina and the devastation of New Orleans. She rarely followed the news and didn't watch much television or read newspapers. She just didn't need to be aggravated by bad news at this point in her life. She seemed fairly stable and content in her room. I continued to wonder why she was in the locked ward when she seemed to be more alert and capable than most of the others.

One week, when I came to visit and give her a massage, she said to me, "There's a man two doors over that I'm very impressed with. He even gave me a kiss once."

My initial comment was, "Good for you, Esther."

Apparently this man was only there temporarily to recover from some condition. He was a part of our conversation for a few weeks.

Esther said, "His name's Roger. He's married and his wife sometimes comes to visit him." Esther beamed with pride when she revealed to me, "Roger told me that he liked me, and that I'm someone very special."

It was cute to see a ninety-some-year-old woman get showered with compliments. Of course, I already knew that Esther was someone very special.

Then one day, I went to see Esther and she wasn't in her room. I worried that she'd died and I wasn't informed. I went to the front desk of the nursing station and asked for Esther. I was told that she'd been moved to a different room. The new room was much bigger and was a corner room. The downside was that there were three beds in the room. At first, only one other bed was occupied. There was also a small bathroom next to the entrance of the room.

Since the nursing home, I tried to go see Esther each Tuesday right after her lunch. By that time, she was all fed and rested and ready to get some therapy. On a couple of occasions, I was there only a few minutes when Esther would look at me painfully and tell me that she needed to go to the bathroom. Fortunately this usually meant that she needed to urinate, and it usually meant that I needed to change her diaper. I could do this, but it involved lifting her out of bed, transferring her to a wheelchair, and wheeling her to the commode. Then I had to remove her old diaper, and after she was finished, I had to put a new diaper on her.

Once, she almost screamed, "BM, BM!"

Mindful of how rough the big African attendants were on Esther, I hurriedly got her to the commode. I never realized how difficult it would be to clean her up and how deep the folds of skin were on her butt. I persevered but vowed that next time, if there was a next time, I'd simply pull the call chain located in the bathroom and get help.

Another annoying thing I didn't really care for was Esther's love affair with corn curls. Charles, her son, visited her almost every day and kept her area stocked with corn curls and soda. The problem was that the curls had the usual orange coating on them, and as she snacked, the coating would build up on her fingers. Sometimes, she even wiped them off on her sheets. There were often sticky yellow food particles all over everything. Once, I asked Charles if he could find a different snack for his mom, but it didn't change anything.

* * *

Esther gave me a break from dealing with my own trauma. By late March, I called a telephone number that I found to get information about a research study at the University of Minnesota. I talked to a nurse who asked me to come to the university and learn more about the study. She gave me directions and set up an appointment. I graduated from the university, so I was familiar with the campus. It'd expanded a lot from when I knew it. I parked in the wrong parking lot, so I wasn't able to get reimbursed for parking the first time. The protocol was explained to me and seemed fairly simple. Each participant was given three drugs to take every evening. One drug was known. Of the other two, one was a placebo and one was an active drug. The study was designed to keep participants from knowing which one was a placebo and which was the real drug. All labs and appointments were free and even parking in the correct lot was free.

Next I talked to the doctor in charge of the study. He tried to dissuade me from entering the study because my white-blood count was still quite good.

He cautioned that once on the drugs, "You'll have to stay on them for life. No one knows what the long-term side effects will be."

I told him my concerns, "Being self-employed, I can't wait until my immune system is damaged irreversibly, leading to other health problems."

The doctor then added, "It's more likely that you'll die from complications of diabetes than from HIV."

I chose to start the program in mid-April. My initial T-cell count starting the program was 386, and my viral load was 56,226. I found the correct parking ramp. That ramp was connected to a long underground tunnel that led to the basement office of the study. I started taking my three meds every evening.

One stipulation I made to the nurse was a request. I asked her, "Is it allowed to continue my nutritional supplements while in the program?"

She answered, "Yes, you can take them, but I need to have a list of all the supplements. I have to check to make sure there won't be any adverse interactions with the new medicines."

I produced this list at the second meeting, and she was a little overwhelmed at its extent.

By the second appointment four weeks later, my T-cells dropped to 355, but my viral load was only 724. I felt as if I was really gaining some ground. But that Memorial Day weekend, I felt like I had a bladder infection. To try a natural approach, I began drinking a lot of cranberry juice. Then my blood sugars got totally out of control. I was starting to get readings in the high 400s and mid 500s. The doctors' offices were closed, and I was reluctant to go to an emergency room because I didn't have insurance. I finally made an appointment Tuesday and saw a partner to my own doctor because mine wasn't going to be there until Wednesday.

I was really disappointed in the partner. He didn't seem to feel there was any concern and only told me to double my diabetes medications. On my way out the door, I made an appointment with my regular doctor for the next day. When I saw him, I told him I thought I had a bladder infection and that maybe I needed insulin. I was having difficulty sleeping and I was losing weight. He checked my urine and gave me antibiotics for an infection. Then he wrote prescriptions for insulin.

I'd never taken insulin before. When I picked up the prescription, I was only given the actual insulin. I was so weak that Art had to drive. He helped me into the drug store. I went all the way home only to discover that I had no mechanism for getting the insulin into my body. We had to go back and get syringes and insulin pens. By then I was exhausted, and my head was spinning from all the sugar in my system. However, none of it was getting to my brain, which needed the sugar to function. I was also losing weight very fast. In a week, I lost twenty pounds and kept losing.

After a few days, my blood sugar stabilized. I kept feeling lethargic and I kept losing weight. My doctor began to write me registered letters about the need for hospitalization. I decided that I was going to have to get insurance somehow. I checked with Minnesota Aids Project and was told about Ryan White funding. I had to register with MinnesotaCare first. I met the income requirements for MinnesotaCare, but there was a stipulation that I couldn't have assets more than ten thousand dollars. I'd just bought my rental house a year earlier, so I was already over that threshold. The woman at the other end of the phone told me that if I didn't qualify for MinnesotaCare, I couldn't apply for Ryan White funding. I was falling through all the cracks.

I also talked to an attorney at Minnesota Aids Project (MAP) to see if I could give my half of the lake property to Art. If I did that, he'd have to pay a sizeable gift tax! Eventually, I decided to apply for Minnesota Comprehensive Health Insurance. This was a program for uninsurable people, so acceptance was guaranteed. I filled out the form, and not knowing what my premium would be, I only gave them my bank account number to access.

Then I waited. I was getting weaker and thinner every day. When I looked in the mirror, I no longer recognized myself and rarely looked in mirrors after that. I kept reading the insurance information that said that it might take up to six weeks to process. I began to get so thin that my pants, even with my belt on, slipped right off of me. I got very weak and then I lost motor power to my right leg. I was developing foot drop. I drove a stick shift, and my right leg no longer responded when I wanted to take my foot off the accelerator and move it onto the brake. Driving became a dangerous chore. I had to move my entire right hip in order to change pressure on the accelerator. I became so weak that I had to rest every ten yards when walking. I had to watch my feet for any uneven surfaces so that I wouldn't trip as my right foot dragged on the ground.

I ate as much as I could, and the amounts should've at least stopped my weight loss. I even stopped at the frozen custard shop on Nicollet Avenue whenever I had a few dollars in my pocket to get a cup of custard. Art bought snack foods that I would've never eaten previously.

I continued to go for my university HIV study. My nurse was becoming more alarmed and contacted my doctor, who pulled me off the study drugs. My T-cell count in June was 382, and my viral load was down to 76. What I clearly remember from those days was the long tunnel walk from the parking lot at the university. It was now such an effort to propel myself through the tunnel. I considered asking for the transport cart, but my pride kept me holding on to the handrails along the corridor and forcing myself to get at least some movement.

I was so weak and tired that everyday activities became difficult. I had to wake a half hour earlier to shave, shower, brush my teeth, and eat breakfast. Even dressing often required more effort than I was able to rally. Sometimes I was still often more than thirty minutes late. When Art and I went grocery shopping, I used the cart as a walker, which seemed therapeutic. I had difficulty lifting the bags of groceries. I was further embarrassed when I met a patient at the store and saw the alarm in his eyes when he noticed how frail I'd become. I came to a new appreciation for the old and the handicapped.

Each week, when I went to visit Esther, it became harder and harder for me to walk up the three flights of steps to her floor. Esther commented on my weight loss. Fortunately she didn't ask me to transfer her to the wheelchair to go to the toilet. Esther could see that I was losing weight and strength.

When I visited, she would pat the side of her bed and say, "It's all right to sit on my bed while you work on me."

I wondered what boundary violations I was committing.

* * *

After four weeks, I called about my insurance status. Only then was I told that I was supposed to have sent a check for the first month. I asked what the amount should be and immediately sent a check. Two more weeks went by and I called again. This time, I was told that since I had a birthday, I moved into a more expensive category and I needed to send an additional check. I sent another check again right away.

By now, I was almost unable to practice chiropractic. I went to work but prayed that I wouldn't have more than two patients with a long rest in between. I had to hold on to the adjusting table to make my way around a patient. I could no longer give a one-hour massage. Once, I was inadvertently locked out of the front door to Art's house. I thought I'd jump the chain-link fence to unlock the back door. I used to be able to jump in one hop just a year ago. This time, I barely got one leg over, and then my pants got caught on the pointed top of the fence. I ripped my jeans as I finally slid over the fence. Another time, I was going to the garage and Art was behind me. My right foot hit the uneven ground and I fell violently straightforward, landing on my hands, knees, and face. I was so humbled. My patients got freaked out at my condition. I'd lost over forty pounds now and looked like a skeleton. Oddly, I retained most of my belly fat.

Now I believed that I was dying from AIDS. I called the insurance company again after eight weeks and was told the second check hadn't been processed yet.

I asked, "Can I hand deliver the check to a real person?"

The woman answered, "Yes, you can."

I got into my car and drove the freeway to Minnetonka. It was scary and dangerous. I pulled into the parking lot. The only vacant parking spot was about 100 yards from the main door. It took me twenty minutes to make my way to the grand edifice. I waited another twenty minutes until a person came to take my check.

Then I asked, "Can you please expedite the process?"

The woman looked at me and curtly replied, "It reads in the instructions that we have six weeks to process each application."

I answered, "Good, so you'll expedite my application because we're going into the eighth week already. You have the forms and the money. All you need to do now is issue me a number."

I checked every day after that to see if I had been assigned an insurance number. Two days later, I had a number, and three days later, my dear friend Nelson drove me to Abbott Northwestern Hospital. I'd never been in a hospital before except maybe to visit someone once or twice in my life. There was some confusion about admitting me, but eventually, they got in touch with my doctor who'd referred me. I was put into a room. It was a new adventure for me. When I was first put in a bed, a nurse welcomed me. Shortly after, a beautiful, blonde thirty-something woman came in to my room and introduced herself to me as my doctor.

I asked, "Where's my usual doctor?"

She explained to me, "He doesn't have privileges at this hospital even though this is the hospital your insurance covers."

One of the first things done was a blood draw. This became a regular thing and seemed to happen every two or three hours.

I joked with the phlebotomist and said, "Maybe I should just take up a bed in the lab so it'd be more convenient for everyone." Then I asked, "Do you have that many vampires living at the hospital who need my blood?"

I learned from Esther that it was important to establish good rapport with all the care attendants and nurses and to address them by their names. I also had to be careful not to be too critical of procedures and doctors and try to allow them to do their best work. I was fairly passive and didn't offer much outside advice.

My doctor returned a few hours later to tell me that my hemoglobin was only five instead of the normal fourteen or better. She ordered three bags of blood, and they were slowly transfused into me. A search began to find where I was losing blood. Blood wasn't found in my urine or stools. Everyone seemed to be puzzled, and I was scheduled for a variety of tests. I was surprised that the hospital food was reasonably good. I'd already stopped all my HIV drugs. I also had to stop my Prandin and metformin for diabetes. I was in renal failure, and my kidneys couldn't process too many drugs. My nurses came to stick me in the morning and then before each meal to determine how much insulin I needed. It became a game I played with my nurses. I'd usually be able to tell within twenty points what my readings were going to be.

I wondered how anyone slept in hospitals. I found out that they dimmed the lights at night. But I'd never been able to sleep on my back before. I had to learn to relax, and eventually I fell asleep. The first night, I was asleep when something woke me up. There was someone in the room with a flashlight. I was startled, but the male nurse quieted me and said he was just checking my monitors. I'd forgotten that I was also hooked up to an EKG monitor with several sticky leads. I fantasized that I'd be assigned a really hot male nurse, who'd find me attractive. Then I thought about my pitiful condition and realized it was only going to happen in my dreams. I kept telling myself that if I see the bright white light, *"Do not go toward it!"*

It was often lonely. I was surprised that I had a private room. I wasn't sure if it was because I was HIV positive or there just happened to be a vacancy. I'd just gotten settled my first day when my cell phone rang and my sister-in-law was on the other end. She called just to say hello, and I told her that I was in the hospital. I was determined not to mention my HIV status to my family unless there was no other choice. She and my brother Jim and their son and daughter-in-law came to visit me the next day. Of course, Art came every day. My friend Nelson stopped by.

I really missed Teddy, my dog. Art told me that Teddy went to my usual chair and stared at it as if to wonder where I was and to ask when I will be back? I think my sister Paula also visited.

Brother Dan called me and asked, "What did they decide was wrong?"

All I said to Dan was, "I am bleeding somewhere. I'm anemic, and they're trying to find out from where."

Even one of Art's sisters and one of his nieces came by.

The blood draws seemed relentless. There was no trace of blood in my stool. I had at least two sets of nurses daily. For the most part, they were very skilled and helpful. On the third day, I had a day nurse, who seemed to have an odd persona. She started the shift and came in angry. I overheard her say something about teenagers and assumed she was talking about her kids.

She left for a while, and when she returned, I asked her, "How old are your kids?"

She looked at me as if I was the crazed one and said, "I don't have any kids, only cats."

Further conversation seemed futile. She reminded me of Kathy Bates in the movie *Misery*. Then she started looking at my arm and messing with the IV. I wondered what she was doing but didn't challenge her. Perhaps she forgot her meds today! Then with little warning, my IV pulled out of my arm, and I began to bleed out. She rushed to get some help, and I probably lost a pint of blood. Help arrived and everything got stabilized. I was afraid of that woman and glad that I never had her again as my nurse.

Finally, an EENT specialist came in and decided to order an endoscopy. He examined me after introducing himself. He acted as if I was an untouchable from India. He washed his hands thoroughly after touching my bedding. I was wheeled from my room to a lab area. I didn't even remember swallowing the camera. Later, it was discovered that I was bleeding in my esophagus. The finding was given to me at the end of the third day. Then, just when I was ready for dinner, the nurse told me that a colonoscopy had been ordered for the next day. I was to have no food, only broth and clear fluids until morning. I argued with the nurse and told her that I was refusing a colonoscopy; I had one two years ago, and I was okay. This went on for about an hour, and I finally told her I was hungry, and I was not having a colonoscopy. If things didn't clear up, I could have one later as an outpatient. I was finally given a regular breakfast the next morning.

After hearing about my esophageal bleeding, a nutritionist was sent to my room. She asked if I knew how to eat. She didn't have any advice about my bleeding and didn't have a clue what foods might be better or worse for my condition. I was told that I would have to take Prilosec every day the rest of my life. I was actually relieved. I didn't have terminal AIDS or cancer. It was only acid reflux. All I had to do is take an antacid the rest of my life, which I could certainly do.

I left the hospital on the fourth day. I felt better and stronger, and even my leg seemed somewhat stronger. Art picked me up. I was happy to get back to see Teddy.

* * *

I went to see Esther again and apologized to her for having to miss a session. She said that she was glad I went to the hospital because I was looking awfully weak. It was a little easier to climb the stairs to see her, but it gradually started to get harder again as the weeks went on.

* * *

Art and I had planned a short vacation to San Francisco and the Wine Country. I thought that it'd be helpful for me to get some rest and relaxation. We flew into San Francisco and rented a car. Then I drove almost all the way to Guerneville on the Russian River. We stopped at a park and looked at some redwoods just north of San Francisco. We continued the drive and got lost around Bodega Bay. My right foot was starting to weaken and show foot drop again. Even though the car was an automatic, my foot became really tired. I finally let Art take the wheel. We arrived at our destination around 10:00 PM in the dark. We were shown to our room and went for a bite to eat. The on-site restaurant was quite expensive. We had a good dinner across the street. Our lodging was all part of a small complex that catered to gays and lesbians. The next morning, we lounged around the pool. My leg was now so bad that my flip-flop wouldn't stay on my right foot when I walked. I was really skinny, and yet I had a large abdomen from my diabetes. We didn't turn any heads from the other gay men. In fact, we felt that people were very aloof and unfriendly.

The next day, we drove to some vineyards and wineries and sampled wine and looked at the countryside. After about six places, we'd only spent three hours, and I was tired and bored. I don't know how anyone can do this all day for several days. We quit and went back to the pool. The next day, we drove back to San Francisco. We found our hotel, unpacked our luggage, returned the car, and then took the BART back to the hotel. We spent a couple of days there. Our highlight was the bus trip that we booked to see the sites, hosted by a tour operator. One night, we walked a lot and got turned around and ended up going miles out of our way. It was up and down hills. The "tenderloin district" was one street over from our hotel. We were warned not to travel through it. It got to be too much for me to navigate all those steep hills. I didn't want to be a drag on poor Art. That night, walking to the hotel, I was often a block behind Art. I wanted to lay down right where I was and cry. I finally made it to our hotel.

By the time we got on the plane, my foot drop was pronounced, and I realized while sitting in my airplane seat that my right foot couldn't flex on its own. It was alarming to me. We got back from our trip, and a few more weeks went by. That same tired feeling was accelerating again. It was harder to climb the steps to visit Esther. Then we went to the Minnesota State Fair, which was one of our traditions. I managed to walk around for three hours and was feeling proud that I hadn't fallen. We were just leaving the gate area when I took my eyes off my feet. I was momentarily distracted. My right foot dragged, and I landed face down on my knees, breaking my fall with my hands. I tore a hole in the knee of my new smaller jeans and had gravel cuts on my hands. Worse for me was that five thousand people witnessed my fall.

By Labor Day, I knew I had to go back to the hospital. I thought I would go my next day off, Wednesday. I went to work that Tuesday. I'd become so weak that I could hardly speak. A massage patient, who happened to be a nurse, called me.

He knew about my HIV status, and when he heard my voice, he said, "David, you have to go back to the hospital. I'm going to call an ambulance."

I said, "Please don't do that because I can't afford an ambulance. I'll have a friend drive me to the hospital."

Then I struggled to put a voice-mail message on the machine. Later, people who called told me that they thought that it might be the last words from me that they'd ever hear. When I called my friend Nelson, who was usually always home, he wasn't. I left him a message and decided I'd have to find a cab to take me. I drove home and got a few things together and sat in my car and called a cab. I looked at the house and wondered if it would be my last vision of it.

Just before the cab arrived, Nelson pulled up and said, "I'm glad I found you in time."

He drove me to the hospital.

Once there, Nelson said, "Can I get you a wheelchair?"

I didn't want to accept defeat so I said, "No, thanks. But I might need help to walk to my room."

Nelson helped me walk to my room. It was in intensive care this time. I was really scared when I was told that I was in ICU. Soon, I was being hooked up to oxygen, EKGs, pulse monitors, and IVs

This time, the admitting doctor came in to take notes. I realized this was my last chance to influence my care.

After a few standard questions, he asked me, "What do you think is going on?"

I pointed to my right kidney area and said, "Something's going on here. I'm feeling a pain. I really think you should take a picture of the area."

Then he said, "What do you think it could be?"

My response was, "I think it might be an aneurysm of my descending aorta."

The doctor was really surprised. He said, "How would you know anything about that?"

I answered, "I am a trained doctor too, and it just seems like a possibility."

He listened to me and ordered a CAT scan for my kidney area.

When the doctor left, the thought occurred to me that sooner or later, I'd have to go to the bathroom. I looked around and realized there wasn't any bathroom nearby. I was hooked up to so many things; I don't know how I'd get out of bed to find one. I rang the call button, and the nurse came and told me that I'd have to use the urinal and the bedpan while I was in ICU. I was also told that I shouldn't use my cell phone.

Not very long after admission, I was wheeled to radiology and readied for a CAT scan. While I was undergoing the exam, I heard gasps.

Someone said, "We've never seen anything so big."

I was removed from the machine and was told that the doctor was going to immediately aspirate a retroperitoneal abscess that was bigger than a large grapefruit. After the initial withdrawal of fluid, two drains were inserted deep into the center of the abscess. I got to drag them around, sticking out of my back for the next two weeks. Small bags collected the draining fluids. The nurse had to irrigate the tubes once or twice daily. During that week alone, they collected over two liters of fluid from the abscess.

I felt better immediately. Of course, I was also getting transfusions because my hemoglobin had dropped to four.

The first nurse exclaimed, "I've never seen anyone able to walk with hemoglobin that low."

I answered, "Did you see me walking? I can hardly walk to a bathroom without resting partway."

The blood draws became so frequent that a PIC line was threaded directly into my subclavian vein so the phlebotomist could easily access my blood through the artificial port. If I needed IVs, they could use the same port. The good part was that I no longer needed any IVs in my arms.

I noticed that Dr. R. came every couple days as he had the first time I was hospitalized. He kept reassuring me that whatever was happening was not HIV related. After I was hooked up to my drains, there wasn't much more to do than to stabilize me. I was given more transfusions. I was also being treated for acute renal failure. But after draining the cyst, I began to gain weight while eating hospital food.

Art visited every day. I knew that this was hard on him. First I had betrayed him, and now it might be up to him to bury me. He mentioned much later that he'd looked at photos and couldn't find any that would work for my funeral. My sister Paula came and brought some beautiful flowers from her yard. Because I was in ICU, I couldn't have them in the room. Nelson called the next day after he dropped me off. He was convinced that I was dying because he was told that I wasn't accepting phone calls and that I was still in ICU. He called the next day and inquired if my family was around standing vigil.

Then the receptionist said, "The family isn't here now, but did you want to talk to him?"

Nelson and I chatted, and I assured him, "I'm already getting better, and the problem's finally been discovered."

After four days, I was moved to a regular private room with a bathroom! I was monitored to make sure my vital signs were strengthening. One evening, a very pleasant Asian man came to my room.

He smiled at me and said, "The doctor wants you to begin walking to get your strength up."

I replied, "The hospital gown doesn't exactly cover me enough for me to be comfortable walking the halls, and I'm not really sure where I am or where I can walk."

He unfolded the fabric in his arms and voila, he showed me the full robe that he'd brought with him.

Then he said gently, "Please put this on and come and walk with me." He had a name tag with a name that I was unfamiliar with.

I asked him, "Where do you come from originally?"

He wanted me to guess. After several futile attempts from me, he said, "I am from Tibet."

So I walked with this angel through the halls of the ward I was in. We stopped at one point, and he went to a small refrigerator and took out two Popsicles. He guided me around and then led me back to my room. He made me realize that I was terribly weak but that if I worked at it, my strength would return.

The following morning, I was awake early as usual. I still had some money in my pants in the closet. I got up and put on my robe and walked past the station nurse.

She looked at me and I said, "I decided to run away this morning."

Her answer was, "Well, you won't get too far dressed like that."

I walked down to the first floor, where there was an in-house McDonalds, and I ordered my first large cup of caffeinated coffee since last Monday. Then I walked back and savored my coffee. Later on, I walked to the gift shop. Soon it'd be Art's birthday, and I wanted to see if there was anything I could buy in the shop that said "birthday." I found a card and a good box of chocolates. That's about all I had money for.

The days started to go by fairly fast. I could watch TV, but daytime programming wasn't very entertaining. I still had a lot of weakness in my right leg, and my balance was shaky. But I finally had a sense of hope, which had eluded me since first hearing my HIV diagnosis. Actually, with all the attention on my kidneys and the cyst, there were moments when I forgot that I was HIV positive. I wasn't taking any medications for it, and no one was mentioning it in relation to my other issues. There was some question about when I would be leaving the hospital. I knew the time was nearing when a specialist came in to remove the PIC from my vein. Then a couple of hours later, the same doctor that admitted me came to go over my discharge. He marveled at the progress that I'd made. He told me he couldn't believe I was the same person he admitted a week earlier.

Then he went over my meds. He had a prescription for Prilosec, insulin, and Prandin that I was again allowed to take. Then he had one more for a sulfa drug. I asked about it because I'd never been on that one before. The doctor told me that during my hospital stay, my T-cells had dropped below 200. Now I fit the definition of full-blown AIDS. Because of it, I had to begin taking sulfa drugs to prevent opportunistic infection. I was shocked back to reality.

It was almost time for dinner, and I was still unsure if I was going to be discharged. Just as I was packing up, I called Art. It was his birthday. He wasn't answering. I left a message. Then a nurse came with all my written records. It was half of a ream of paper. Art called back just as my dinner was being delivered. I wolfed down the food and then waited outside in the sun for Art. As I sat there, I remembered the vase of flowers from Paula and went back to collect it. It was a lot of walking for me with several odd pieces of luggage. I got back out front as Art pulled up. He helped me into the truck with everything. I was finally going back to our home, which I thought I'd never see again.

Chapter Thirty-Six

Reality Check

On the way to the house, we drove to the pharmacy and filled the prescriptions. I couldn't wait to get home and see Teddy. He was really happy to see me.

It felt so good to be home. I had two drain tubes stuck in my back. I was supposed to leave them in for one more week. After that, I was scheduled to get a follow-up CAT scan to see the progress of the cyst. I was told that a home health-care nurse would come by daily to irrigate the tubes. The following morning, I wondered how that was going to happen. No one had made any firm arrangements for the home nurse. I looked through the stack of discharge papers and found a number for my social worker. I called her, and she offered to set up something. She was to call me back but never did. That afternoon, I received a call from a home nurse, who said she'd come out yet today but wasn't sure exactly when it would be.

At seven at night, a small car pulled up, and a huge woman attempted to get out with some distress. She came to the door and showed her credentials.

Then she announced, "You aren't on my list, and I'm not sure what I was supposed to be doing for you."

I decided to escort her to the front door and told her, "I don't want you working with me if you aren't sure what your orders are."

The next day, I called the social worker again, and I was told that my insurance wouldn't cover the home irrigations unless I was homebound. I'd been going to my office every day, hoping to start up my business again.

I stated, "Either my tubes need irrigation or they don't. I can come to the hospital if need be." It was never going to happen.

My fourth day home with the tubes, I got ready to go to my office. I got in my car and drove the two miles to my office. When I tried to exit the car, one tube got stuck, and as I got out of the car, the whole tube pulled out of my back. I had pus on my T-shirt and wasn't sure if this was a medical emergency or not. I put in a call to home care but didn't get a return call. I went through my day with a wet shirt. It didn't seem to do any harm. I was having trouble sleeping because I couldn't toss and turn with the tubes in my back. Two days after the first tube came out, I yanked the second one out. Then I could finally sleep in any position.

When I went for my CAT scan, the admitting nurse asked, "Where are the tubes that you're supposed to have in your back?"

I admitted to her, "I got tired of them so I pulled them out. The tubes weren't flushed as they're supposed to be anyway."

I had the CAT scan. Then I got a call from my doctor.

He said, "The cyst wasn't resolved, and more tubes might have to be inserted again."

I said to him, "If the tubes aren't going to be properly maintained, I'm not having them put back in."

Late that day, he called me back after a consult with the surgeon. The surgeon seemed to think the progress was good, and I didn't need any more tubes. It was suggested that I stay on antibiotics an extra week.

This last surgeon and doctor consult with follow up CAT scan was sent to my insurance as HIV related, which it wasn't. Later I got an extra bill for three thousand dollars that I was supposed to pay because the insurance was new and didn't cover preexisting conditions. At this point, I tried to fight it, but I gave up because no one wanted to change the wording of the diagnosis. I was drowning in debt already because I was without much work all summer. I kept going deeper into ready reserve.

* * *

I was anxious to get back to the university study. I called my nurse contact, and she told me that two of my doctors asked to have me unblinded from the drug study.

She explained, "The process to unblind you already started. Ultimately it means that you'll be dropped from the study."

I told her, "I can't afford the medications and blood testing on my own, and I don't want to be unblinded."

She said, "You have to call your doctors and tell them you want the process stopped before it's too late."

Apparently, I just made the deadline. I was able to get back into the study in the fall of 2006.

Less than a month after being discharged from the hospital, my T-cells had rebounded to 365, but my viral load was over 27,400. I enjoyed meeting with my nurse.

I asked her, "Do you think I should continue on my sulfa drugs?"

She answered, "I can't tell you to stop, but if it were me, I would stop those drugs."

So I did. The long walk through the tunnel was my measure of improvement for my paralyzed right leg. It was very slow to come back. I invented my own rehab exercises that I did several times a day. I actually had to learn how to walk all over again. It took nearly a year to get close to my normal stride. I still feel weakness if I get stressed out or when I'm overly tired.

* * *

Life doesn't stop just because you almost died. When I was in the hospital the first time, I received a letter from the city about my investment property. I was cited for a garage that needed paint, and it was also determined that my driveway off the alley had to be either black topped or more gravel was needed on the surface. I was given eight weeks to comply with the order. I didn't have any money to carry out the order. I also didn't have the energy to attempt to do the work myself. Then when I went into ICU, I wasn't sure that I'd be alive to care about the order anyway. I ignored the order, and of course, I was then fined two hundred dollars for failure to comply.

My good tenant moved out when I tried to sell the property, and the house sat vacant when I was in ICU. I had a lawn sign posted, showing my cell phone number. I wasn't supposed to use my cell phone in ICU, but a woman, T, called me there. She explained that her mother lived nearby, and she passed the house daily. She was really interested in renting it. I told her that I'd call her back after I was out of the hospital. I thought that it would be better to have someone in the house than let it go vacant. T knew exactly how to go under my radar, and she started living in the house even before she gave me a security deposit and the full first-month rent. It turned out to be another disaster.

In late September, I found a man who agreed to top my driveway with asphalt. I only had about two thousand dollars left on my credit card, and he bid just under that. Then before it got too cold, Art and I painted the garage. I still had to appear before the tribunal to plead for my two-hundred-dollar fine back. I got that back.

Then the following year, I ended up going to court to get T out of the house after losing several months rent. The house was heavily damaged from the woman, who turned out to be a crack-cocaine prostitute and who invited several of her Johns to move in with her. But that's another story.

* * *

In November 2006, I was starting to build my business all over again. It was slow. I stopped going to the Internet since I found out about my HIV status. There was still an addiction, but now I didn't fit any definitions of what other men desired. I was old, diseased, unfit, depressed, and damaged. I didn't want to encourage the spread of the virus. I was actually fearful that some postings that advertised as positive-friendly were traps to lure diseased men to their deaths. I decided that I was going to tell patients about my HIV status only on an as-needed, case-to-case basis.

I began to see Esther again. She noticed that I was finally gaining my strength and weight back. It was around that time that Esther was moved again. She was finally put in a corner room outside the locked ward. She only had one roommate at first. Not too long after, the third bed was filled.

I said to Esther one time, after I saw some of the bills from the hospital, "My hospital stay alone cost $154,000."

She simply said, "Well, I think it's worth it because you're alive."

I later discovered that my insurance only had to pay forty-eight thousand dollars to cover the full amount.

* * *

A couple of weeks before Thanksgiving, one of my long-time patients came in for a treatment. I've been seeing her and her family for more than twenty-five years. She didn't usually come very often, and she hadn't seen me while I was so sick and weak. I saw her twin sister during that time, however. Her sister relayed my poor condition to her. I gave her a good treatment, and when she came out to pay for her visit, she reached into her purse and produced a check, which she handed to me. I looked at the check. It was a check for ten thousand dollars. I was confused, surprised, shocked. I asked her what it meant.

She said to me, "My husband and I are millionaires. We heard about your horrible summer and your loss of business. We talked it over, and we want this to be our gift to you."

I cried. I couldn't believe it. I didn't even know they were millionaires.

I told her, "I can't tell you how thankful I am to you. It is so generous. It's too much!"

She calmly said, "And what do I owe you for today?"

Chapter Thirty-Seven

Full Circle

I had a lot to be thankful for that Thanksgiving 2006. I was alive. I had my little Teddy. I had generous, caring patients. Through all the turbulence, Art and I were still together. While we had a lot to work through, my practice was growing and could only get better from what it was in August. Esther was still a good friend.

It was just before Christmas that year that I decided to write a book. At first, I wanted to document my life by writing everything that I could remember. That's about the time that I told Esther that I was going to write a book.

I still recoil from hearing the comatose woman say, "It won't be worth reading."

After everything I went through, I feel that God or the universe or whatever one believes in works in mystical ways. I felt it was important for me to write a book.

* * *

I began my university HIV routine in earnest. I didn't like some of the side effects of the HIV drugs. I often had runny stools; I had occasional severe foot and leg cramps. My mild diabetic neuropathy got much worse. My blood pressure began to rise, and my triglycerides were off the charts. When I first began with the drugs, I was warned about vivid dreams.

Back then, I asked the nurse, "You mean more vivid dreams than usual?"

The dreams were very bizarre, but I found them enjoyable most of the time. I didn't like the feeling that my brain never slept. I took the drugs just before I lay down to sleep. If I didn't fall asleep right away, the drugs would get into my system and keep my brain active the whole night. Once in a while, the dreams would be very dark and sinister. I would even call them disturbing. Some participants had to change drugs because of this effect.

My nurse was very encouraging. She was also blinded about which drugs I was actually on.

A few times, she mentioned, "Whichever drugs you're taking, you're doing better than anyone else in the study."

I enjoyed my visits to the university and monitored my progress with my leg paralysis by how much my walk down the long tunnel improved. It seemed strange that at fifty-six years old, I had to learn how to walk all over again.

My task at hand now was to experiment with nutritional supplements to minimize the undesirable side effects of the HIV meds. I was already on many different things because of my diabetes. I attended a seminar in 2004, which was presented by a clinical nutritionist. It was devoted to nutritional help for diabetic patients. He offered good reasons why certain supplements were helpful. I've since been taking most of the things he recommended. Many of these supplements spill over in dealing with HIV. While I don't believe every regimen works identically in all individuals, through trial and error, I've found the one that seems to work for me.

I also enjoy cooking and place a high value on spices as medicinal adjuncts. These spices seem more effective for my diabetes than for HIV. But I now spend time, money, and effort in discovering new combinations of food and spices that have health effects equal to pharmaceuticals.

I've always thought that a person's whole body health was the reflection of the health and happiness of each of the trillions of cells that make up that body. From my studies in histology, I've made a goal to try to keep all my cells active, useful, and fulfilled in purpose. I look at my body as my own universe. If my cells are happy and working together in harmony, I'll be healthy. One also has to deal with toxic cell-waste products, which build up in a body. Antioxidants help with that. I use my memory of things that I read about, like beneficial effects of various foods, and adapt my taste to accommodate those foods. I have forty years of accumulated information and try to use it to my best advantage. I'm sure that I sometimes drive Art crazy with my unusual eating combinations.

When I first got out of the hospital, I was able to regulate my diabetes without insulin again. By 2007, I started using long-acting insulin once in the evenings. I also take a combined nutritional supplement specially formulated for diabetes. And of course, I still take Prandin thirty minutes before a meal. But that keeps me around 6.5 when I check my hemoglobin A1C. Below 7 is acceptable for me.

I've had several middle-aged patients come in to my office distressed over their weight gains and fearful that being overweight would lead to diabetes. They are guilt ridden. I try to comfort him or her.

I usually say to them, "If fat caused diabetes, every fat person would be diabetic. They're not. Excess fat is a result of diabetes, not the cause."

Another way that I deal with my diabetes is to avoid alarm by becoming detached from my blood sugar numbers. I monitor but only to make decisions as to what course I should follow during the rest of my day.

Diabetes is the least of my concerns now. I have been diabetic ten years, and its management is fairly simple for me now. It is interesting for me that a correlation seems to exist, at least for me, between diabetes and HIV. When my HIV labs show my viral load as undetectable, my diabetes is more easily managed. By March of 2007, I finally got to an undetectable viral load. My T-cell count was 482 then. I was faithful to the study drugs and never missed any doses. It was hammered into me that missed dosages could allow the virus to mutate, forming viruses that would then be resistant to the current drugs. Indeed this has happened to many HIV-positive people.

* * *

In 2007, I continued to visit Esther. While 2006 was my awful year, 2007 was Esther's. She was in a large corner room that initially had only one other bed. It was a bright room with a view of the freeway. Her first roommate was the woman who always seemed to be in a coma. Early in the year, Esther told me that someone stole her glasses. Now she was only able to see large objects and people's faces. She could no longer read.

Once I came to visit and she wasn't in her bed. I found her in the dining area, sitting at a table. Esther was confused and disoriented. She thought that I was her son, Charles. I helped her back to bed but didn't treat her that day. Another time, she asked me to call the police.

She told me a wild story, that someone who knew both her and Charles was taking money from both of them. I should try to call the police and tell them to intervene. I kept asking her questions to try to clarify the story.

I asked her, "Why doesn't Charles call the police?

None of it seemed to be real so I tried to humor her. Esther continued with this story for almost a month. Finally, one day when I arrived, Esther had a smile on her face.

According to her, "The police caught the crook red-handed. He's in jail now. Everyone's going to get all their money back."

I was relieved. I still don't know if the whole thing was imaginary or real. I suspect the former.

Then I came one afternoon, and Esther looked even older than her real ninety-five. She was having difficulty eating and speaking.

Finally, she said, "My daughter-in-law took my dentures."

That explained why her face was so sunken. I wondered if the staff had suggested removing them so that Esther wouldn't choke. Esther seemed to be going downhill, but she still was conversational. She even told me that her favorite brother, Calvin, died after a couple years of dealing with cancer. She repeated that story for several weeks.

She became reflective and often said, "After all, I've lived a long and interesting life."

Esther told me several years ago that she'd had all of her funeral arrangements paid in advance.

Esther got a new roommate that spring. She was a heavyset woman, who appeared to be much younger than Esther. The first time I walked in and saw her, the new woman was sitting in a wheelchair, watching a small portable TV. She talked loudly, usually to herself. She always seemed to be in a dither. I busied myself with Esther, and the new person, Doris, would drop a pencil or her remote control and ask me to retrieve them for her. I was annoyed at the interference. Then, even more annoying, I looked over and saw a puddle forming under her wheelchair. When an attendant came in, I pointed out the urine puddle under the wheelchair. It took the staff almost an hour before it was cleaned up. Of course, they also had to change the diaper on Doris. This wasn't an isolated incident, and I witnessed a puddle under her wheelchair many times after that. Nelson and I gave Doris a new name—Puddles.

I asked Esther one day what she thought about Doris. I was surprised to hear Esther say that she liked her. Esther enjoyed the liveliness Puddles brought to the room. When late summer came, I brought some garden-ripe cherry tomatoes to Esther. She put one in her mouth. I forgot that she didn't have teeth any more. Esther kept the tomato in her mouth the entire hour and spit it out just as our session was ending. I gave the rest of the tomatoes to Puddles.

* * *

Early in 2007, Brenda, my nurse from the university, told me that funding was being cut from the HIV study that I was in. The initial study was nationwide and administered through the National Institute of Health. Several states were having their entire funding cut off. Participants were supposed to access programs in surrounding states. Brenda noted that Hawaii was being cut and openly wondered which bordering states those folks were supposed to go to for help. She told me as a heads-up that while the program was originally set up to be ongoing, it seemed like it would be prematurely terminated at some point. The university would try to keep it going as long as possible.

* * *

I started to paint the outside of my house/office that year. I chose a soft yellow and painted the trim white. It improved the property immensely. Later that year, I was able to refinance and use some home equity to pay down bills. Patients trickled in. I was still tempted to go to my old addictive Web sites. My relationship with Art had changed. The intimate sexual exchanges were gone. We had arguments, and there were times when I thought I should try to find another positive man to share my life with. But I loved Art. We'd been a couple for twenty years. I really didn't want to start all over with an unknown person and all their baggage. I started writing. With that and painting my house, I was able to fill my free time and then some.

* * *

When I got so weak and sick in the spring 2006, I quit my volunteer work at Aliveness Project. I'd been doing that for twenty years. It opened up my Monday evenings. I tried to visit the old group a few times, usually on my day off. It always seemed that the people I knew weren't there at the time I visited. I felt displaced, unrecognized, and unneeded. I didn't join the Project as a member, even though I now qualified for membership. I still had some denial about my own HIV status. I didn't feel or think that I appeared sick. Actually, I felt fortunate that other than my episode with my cyst, which I was told was not HIV related, I've never experienced any HIV-related symptoms.

Now my concerns were avoiding the awful side effects of the HIV drugs. After working closely with many HIV-positive people, I was well aware of some of the downsides of the medications. The newer drugs had been tweaked and bundled together in ways to minimize some bad effects. Still, long-term survivors seemed to have a lot of skeletal and heart issues. I knew that my intake of calcium needed to double to accommodate the drugs. A close friend of mine had to have bilateral hip replacement. His HIV drugs hardened the bone cells and circulation to those hipbone cells. The cells died because they didn't get the blood supply that they needed to live. Others were having compression fractures in their spines.

Another issue is that many HIV medications cause high triglycerides and heart disease, which increases the likelihood of death by heart attack. When I brought up some of these things to my medical doctors, the prevailing attitude seemed to be that people who where HIV positive should feel lucky to live long enough to need hip replacements and have heart attacks.

* * *

The field was wide open for the coming presidential elections in 2008. Sometimes, Esther was lucid enough to comment on her favorite—Hillary Clinton. Esther wanted to have a woman president elected before she died. I didn't want to say much because I was leaning toward Obama. One day, I came to visit, and Esther was staring out her big window.

She pointed and said to me, "Look at the big red barn, it's just like the barn that we had in Chaska growing up. They're doing the fall chores."

I looked. Other than a somewhat large garage on the other side of the freeway, I didn't see anything that looked like a farm. I knew that Esther was coming to the end of her life. We talked about when she was a little girl, who worked and played with her brothers and sisters. I tried to get her ready to go home again.

I continued to visit Esther for several more weeks. It seemed to me that she was slipping away gradually. The conversations got shorter and more focused on her early life. She slept a lot more. Then one of the last times I visited, she slept through most of the session. Esther didn't direct me to the drawer where Charles would leave a check for me. I came one last time in November 2007, and Esther was deep in sleep. I decided not to wake her. We'd already said good-bye to each other during the October visits. I left the nursing home and vowed not to return unless Charles insisted. I called Charles and asked him that if it was all right with him if I wasn't going to visit his mother again.

Chapter Thirty-Eight

A Learning Curve

Art and I made our usual trip to St. Martin in 2008. As always, we ran into several of our time-share friends, who are at The View the same weeks. It seemed as though someone or other was struggling with health issues. It was always a good marker to check in with each other once a year. I felt as though Esther had checked out already. Before I left for vacation, I went online to the obituaries, but she wasn't listed yet. Once I came so close to death myself, my priorities and concerns shifted. I didn't want to waste my life by getting caught up in petty day-to-day struggles. Life was too valuable to me now.

I was hopeful that with Bush nearing his end, things could finally start to get better. Several of the older women came to visit when I was at the pool. They're all avid readers, and many wondered how my book was coming along. I had to tell them that I was still working on it.

I was becoming obsessed about trying to explain to myself my irrational behavior of computer sexual addiction. How could I be so impulsive and irresponsible to engage in dangerous unprotected sex with strangers? I felt shame every time I even considered telling anyone of my status. I felt very undesirable and tainted. My own self-image of being a model of health for my patients was shattered. Because I was on drugs that caused my mind to be active much of the night, it only made my obsessions worse. It was embarrassing and humiliating to read the statistics for HIV and to realize that I was one of only six people in Minnesota over the age of fifty to be diagnosed with HIV in 2006.

* * *

I recall a test I took in my Psychology 101 class that I took with over three thousand other students thirty-five years ago. A question on the test referred to a type of reward that would cause behavioral addiction. Thinking of Pavlov and the salivating dogs, I answered "consistent reward." I got the question wrong and asked the teaching assistant why my answer was wrong. He explained to me that consistent reward would result, over time, in extinguishing the behavior because boredom would eventually set in. B.F. Skinner showed that intermittent reward (irregular reward) was what caused the behavior modifications of addiction. I know that from training my dogs. If I give them the treat every single time, they get sloppy and bored. If I reward them most of the time but once in a while skip a treat, they become more predictable in their response.

In 1977, I worked a summer in a gay hotel in Atlantic City before it became famous for gambling. Down the block, toward the boardwalk was an old-fashioned arcade. I went inside and watched a live chicken, which was kept in a glass cage. I spent hours watching the hen and wondered if she was going to get enough food. To play the game with the chicken, one put a quarter in the slot machine. This triggered a small ball that looked like a ping-pong ball to come down a chute. The chicken would take the ball and shoot a basket into the tiny hoop inside the cage. Once the chicken made the basket, a pellet of food appeared and the hen got some food. I wondered why the chicken didn't get bored, revolt, and stop responding. I worried that the chicken might starve if too few people paid the quarter.

One day, the keeper of the chicken came by, and I asked him, "Why doesn't the chicken get bored and stop making baskets?"

He replied, "If you watch closely, you'd notice that every once in a while, the food pellet failed to drop. This makes the chicken more determined to make a basket the next time and causes the chicken to become addicted to the behavior."

Acknowledging that I have an impulsive nature, often suffer from low self-esteem, and shame of being unable to provide for myself, it all figures into this behavior modification and addiction theory. Not that there's any rational excuse for my downfall. But I began to understand how the computer was able to lure me into behavior that I should've been able to resist. I began to look at other addictions and realized that gambling, substance abuse, and even cigarette smoking may also have strong behavioral components involving inconsistent rewards. These types of reward are often minimized because of biochemical and physiological explanations. Why would anyone smoke twenty cigarettes to have their lungs plugged up with pollution and risk cancer? I think it's because once in a great while, the reward of smoking the perfect pleasurable cigarette reinforces the few other really great smokes in their life. Junkies shoot up to try to find that perfect high that they got once but rarely get anymore. The singer Sade has a song, "It's Never as Good as the First Time." I love that song, and she's right—one has to enjoy the moment and stop trying to recreate old memories because it never happens exactly the same way twice.

With this insight, I started to make adjustments to the road toward forgiveness. My health would never improve until I quit beating myself up over my mistakes. Of all the diseases in the world, being infected with the HIV virus is one of the most shameful. Americans, in particular, are quick to define HIV infection as a moral defect. It doesn't do those exposed any good to frame HIV in shame. I beat myself up a thousand times for being so foolish. But I had to get beyond that. After all, a cigarette smoker should also know that their behavior is a risk for poor health and cancer. Why is that so different from unprotected sex?

* * *

After we got back from St. Martin, I was busy at work. It was several weeks later that I went online again to search the obituaries. When I did, I discovered that Esther died on Valentine's Day 2008 at the age of 96. I was sad that the obituary didn't mention her adopted son, Charles. It was very brief and was probably written by the funeral home director. Esther had been a valuable friend. She gave me unconditional love when I needed it most.

Esther made me realize that in the big picture, we will all die eventually. It's all part of being human. It's also important to live a full and generous life. It's okay to have our own opinions, but we should live our lives with honesty and charity. We can't always prevent our bodies from wear, tear, and disfigurement. Our bodies are only the vessels that we live from. Death is the final equalizer. Esther was secure with herself. She had a strong sense of self-esteem. I'll always miss her.

* * *

I could tell that I was getting stronger as I walked through the tunnel from the university parking lot to the study suite. My numbers kept improving, and my viral load was undetectable now for nearly a year. My T-cells varied from the high 400s to the low 600s. My only concerns were that my doctor wanted to put me on medications to control high blood pressure and also another drug for my high triglycerides. I told him that I didn't want to chase side effects with even more drugs. Eventually I relented and started both new drugs. At least they were generic and inexpensive. By July of 2008, Brenda notified me that the HIV program was ending. She told me that George Bush had signed an executive order ending all the federal funding for the NIH program. My last visit was to be October 10. I was given the last of my drugs in July. Brenda mentioned that I should bring any unused drugs back to her on my final visit. Then she whispered that if I forgot, they couldn't do anything about it.

I didn't immediately understand the full impact that the ending of the program would have on me. I'd soon be forced to purchase my own drugs and to pay for all of my lab tests. I had insurance for which I was paying around five hundred dollars a month. What was difficult to comprehend was that my HIV drugs were going to cost $1800 a month! Every lab appointment was going to be nine hundred dollars. I was barely keeping up with insurance and other living expenses. Now suddenly I had to pay three hundred dollars a month more for the drug co-pay, and I also had to start paying for my labs tests. Only after I paid three thousand dollars would I be fully covered by my insurance.

It seemed like an insurmountable sum of money to me. If I could grow my business a little more, I would almost make the new amounts needed. However, that also depended on the economy turning around quickly. It would be a daunting task.

It was November 2008 that my benefactors came to my rescue again. Richard came in for treatment and talked about Qigong and Master Lin. Richard wanted me to go see Master Lin to eliminate my diabetes. I hadn't told him yet about HIV. When I hesitated because of money concerns, Richard signed over a set of ten gift certificates to see Master Lin. Of course I would go if my visits were paid for. So I began my Qigong experience.

I've always been interested in alternative healing. I was excited to try this ancient healing technique. It was quite a drive to the suburbs, but one that I grew to enjoy. I felt as if I was in a very relaxing and nonjudgmental realm. Each session started with an associate. The last ten minutes, Master Lin would enter and make assessments and add his expertise. There were many audio CDs and other aids to meditation. I bought a few and enjoyed using them as therapy at home.

The night after my first session, I woke up drenched with sweat. I was having a nightmare. I was crying and kept repeating, "I don't have AIDS."

After only four visits, Master Lin said to me, "I can no longer detect the virus in you."

I wasn't sure how to take this. I'd been testing undetectable for almost a full year already by Western medical standards. I went home and searched the Internet for any mention of healings and cures. I found nothing. After another week, I decided that I would take a leap of faith. I stopped my HIV meds on Thanksgiving 2008. A month later, I had my regular blood work done, and my viral load remained undetectable. I continued to see Master Lin through the next three months.

That January, I was excited to go to St. Martin. I felt that maybe I was cured of HIV. I felt very good and I was off my medications. I thought that maybe I had the perfect ending for my book. I had a new appreciation of St. Martin, and I was so happy to be there and maybe in really good health. I'd been thinking about a tattoo for several years, but now I knew what I wanted the tattoo to look like. I wanted to honor Master Lin with a colorful yin and yang symbol at the base of my spine. I couldn't get it before St. Martin because a new tattoo needed protection from the sun, so I decided to have it done right after I got back. I got my tattoo in early March.

In mid-March, I felt nervous. What if the virus decided to reappear? I went ahead and got my tattoo a week before my next blood tests. I saw Master Lin a few days before the blood tests. Then I had the tests and a few days after that, I got the results. I was sorry to find out that my viral load had jumped to 136,000! I felt as though Master Lin should've known and told me that he felt the virus coming back. Perhaps he decided that it would be negative information to me.

I had no alternative but to begin my HIV medications again. I had several months' worth stockpiled. So that's what I did. I wasn't happy with the routine. I began to think about pharmaceutical companies in a competitive market place.

To me, it sounds crazy to have the same type of competition to make big profits for companies who should be helping people to become healthy. I know mostly about HIV medications, which have a short history. I'm sure the same thing goes on with diabetes, cancer, organ transplant, and other dramatic diseases. In Minnesota alone in 2010, there are over five thousand people living with HIV. If most of them are on medications, 5,000 x $1800 = $9,000,000. The pharmaceutical industry is making at least nine million dollars for providing life-saving drugs to Minnesotans every month. This is a captive audience. It also seems ironic that out of four or five drug companies and about at least that number of options, all combinations of HIV drugs seem to cost $1800 a month. I'm all for making profit and free trade, but that's not what's operating here. There's price fixing and a seventeen-year (patent rights) monopoly. I know there are research costs, but why are millions also being spent in advertising when there are so few other alternatives? Why would companies improve the current drugs if they were assured huge profits from the existing drugs? To me, it all seems outrageous.

Our current medical model is broken. Health care is in competition to come up with the most expensive way to treat disease so that big business can create the most profits for their companies. Ironically, many other nations provide free HIV drugs for their citizens. Canada and Brazil are two examples that I'm aware of. This American model only promotes high recurring costs for the sick and huge profits for drug companies and hospitals, rather than provide a cure for disease.

My hopes for a cure have been dashed. However, I often think about what I've learned. Two important findings immediately come to mind. Qigong allowed me to lose my fear of the virus that seems to dominate Western medicine. But perhaps the most important thing that Master Lin gave to me was to show me the power of love and forgiveness in the healing process. It's Qigong that opened my eyes to the idea that in order to love anyone else, I need to love myself. For two and a half years, I'd beat myself up, loathed myself, and wallowed in humiliation and shame. Now I'm finally aware of how important it is to love myself. Love is a powerful tonic for illness. I also have to forgive myself for making errors in judgment. I have to put my mistakes behind me and learn from them. Of course, I also learned the power of meditation.

Esther knew the power of love intuitively. She loved me unconditionally and was never bitter about her own ending. Esther never seemed to have much fear either. I think that's why I got along with her so well. We both enjoyed adventure and didn't let fear dictate our lives. She was always eager to learn. In my opinion, it's important to try to keep learning your entire life. It's also important to live your life with as little fear as possible. No one advances if we allow fear to stop us in gridlock.

Addictions can be a powerful force. I believe we all have addictions. Not every addiction is unhealthy. But like the chicken, sometimes we can find ourselves caged in glass as a result of our fear and low self-esteem. We need courage and maybe even outside help to break the glass cage that can imprison us.

Currently, I'm on my own protocol of taking my HIV meds, one month on and then one month off. I save a lot of money, and I've been able to protect my body from the worst side effects of medications. I've maintained low viral loads and high T-cell counts. My doctor was skeptical at first, but he's become curious lately because of my success. I take Chinese herbs for my immune system as well as many different nutritional supplements that I keep in an old shoebox. I have a lot of energy. I'm working harder on growing my chiropractic practice and writing.

I think of Esther often and thank her for helping me to find love and life without the constraints of fear. She was a rudder and a mentor for me, and she really helped me navigate through my many midlife crises. I'm also grateful to Esther because she infected me with her strong self-esteem.

Conclusion

Life doesn't always follow the path that one expects it to. Stages of life are different for everyone. For me, midlife is the time in my life when I was invited to become a true member of the sea of humanity. Once one reaches that sea, there's finally a perspective of life, a big picture view, which is less contentious. Competition between scarce resources can finally give way to cooperation and coexistence within a collective. With the joint efforts of all humanity, formidable obstacles can be overcome.

A virus causes AIDS. Viruses also cause warts, cancer, flu, and shingles. But HIV is only a virus. A virus is an incomplete life form that must hijack a living cell in order to reproduce. It lives a symbiotic lifestyle, totally dependent on healthy human cells. Eradication hasn't worked very well as a method of viral elimination. Coexistence may be a better option until a real cure is found. Perhaps with more information about the AIDS virus, we can get to a place of perception to see HIV as a nuisance, which can be accommodated, rather than as an enemy that needs to be destroyed.

Of course, most of all, I'd like people to stay active in pursuing ways of becoming virus free. My hope is that a way will be found to achieve that goal. In order to do this, we may have to turn the page or go to the next chapter. We need to tap the entire reservoir of human experience and knowledge to decode the complex riddle of the AIDS virus. In order to have the best access to this reservoir, we need to try to overcome our vulnerabilities by working to achieve higher self-esteem and self-respect. This is the only way we can begin to love and respect others and to share their expertise.

It's helped me immeasurably to tap into my magical thinking from time to time, to frame my perceptions of reality so that I'm better able to overcome the challenges of my life.

The End